WELCOME

If Covid-19 taught us anything, it was to not take travel for granted – get out there and see the world while you still can! And you don't even have to go very far...
Europe is full of fascinating history, great food, even better wine, stunning scenery, wild nightlife, retail and incredible beaches, – you just need to know where to look. From the ever popular capitals to lesser known hidden gems, let *European City Breaks* inspire you to explore all the delights this eclectic continent has to offer (whatever your tastes) and book your weekend away, today!

CONTENTS

TOP TIPS
- 06 Planning your journey
- 10 Top Cities
- 18 Map

NORTH
- 22 Bergen
- 24 Tromso
- 25 Oslo
- 26 Stockholm
- 28 Gothenburg
- 29 Turku
- 30 Helsinki
- 32 Copenhagen
- 33 Aarhus
- 34 Reyjavik
- 35 Vilnus
- 36 Tallinn
- 37 Riga

SOUTH
- 40 Rome
- 42 Milan
- 43 Parma
- 44 Florence
- 45 Bologna
- 46 Cremona
- 48 Naples
- 49 Matera
- 50 Venice
- 52 Palermo
- 53 Seville
- 54 Barcelona
- 56 Valencia
- 57 Palma De Mallorca
- 58 San Sebastián
- 59 Madrid
- 60 Bilbao
- 61 Porto
- 62 Lisbon
- 64 Athens
- 65 Kavala
- 66 Thessaloniki
- 67 Valletta

30

58

EAST & CENTRAL

- 70 Krakow
- 72 Warsaw
- 73 Torun
- 74 Prague
- 75 Bucharest
- 76 Brasov
- 77 Sibiu
- 78 Bratislava
- 79 Budapest
- 80 Sarajevo
- 81 Belgrade
- 82 Pristina
- 83 Kotor
- 84 Ljubjana
- 85 Koper
- 86 Skopje
- 87 Zagreb
- 88 Dubrovnik
- 89 Sofia
- 90 Istanbul
- 91 Tiblisi

WEST

- 94 London
- 96 Brighton
- 97 Liverpool
- 98 York
- 99 Manchester
- 100 Bristol
- 102 Cardiff
- 103 Dublin
- 104 Belfast
- 105 Edinburgh
- 106 Stirling
- 107 Glasgow
- 108 Amsterdam
- 110 Rotterdam
- 111 Bruges
- 112 Brussels
- 113 Vienna
- 114 Salzburg
- 115 Bern
- 116 Zurich
- 117 Hamburg
- 118 Munich
- 119 Freiburg Im Breisgau
- 120 Berlin
- 122 Luxembourg
- 123 Nice
- 124 Paris
- 126 Lyon
- 127 Bordeaux
- 128 Nimes

PLANNING A EUROPEAN CITY BREAK

A BIT OF PREPARATION MEANS YOU CAN RELAX AND ENJOY YOUR VACATION, WHETHER IT'S A LONG WEEKEND OR A LEISURELY WEEK-LONG HOLIDAY

TOP TIPS

Picking a destination
Things to consider...
Time of year: Weather can make or break a holiday, so check out the climate before you book. Check for festivals and events that cause a city to be busier and more expensive than normal; school holidays are sometimes best swerved if you want to avoid queues and crowds.
Specific events: You may well be going to a city for a specific reason and if this is the case, check your dates and the availability of tickets before you book your flights.
Seasonal variations: It may be appealing to visit a city when it's quieter but it's good to do a bit of research into whether all the things you want to see are still open in the low season.
What ticks your boxes? Tailor your city break to what you love and it's bound to be a success. Check out our top cities for every passion on page 10 for our recommendations of the best cities for fans of history, arts and culture, food, nature, shopping and even nightlife! Whether you are itching for a unique destination to party with your pals or an artsy, relaxing city where you can soak up the local culture – you are sure to find a spot you haven't even considered yet.

Where could your passions take you next?

"Tailor your city break to what you love"

Transport
Things to consider...
- Airlines vary their schedules depending on the season. If you're going on a city break in the low season you can save money, but you may find that you can only fly out on a Tuesday and return on a Saturday, which may not fit your plans if you're wanting to make it a weekend break.
- Flight duration and time difference in the destination country can make a difference when it comes to a short break. Transfer times are another key factor in the decision process.
- You can end up with an extra day for exploring if you take an earlier flight. Likewise, on the return leg, an evening flight gives you an extra day in the city. The other bonus of taking flights at what some might consider unsociable hours is that they're often cheaper – leaving more money for souvenirs/culture/tapas/spa treatments (delete as appropriate)!
- Double-check the baggage allowance when booking flights and bear in mind that ensuring you can fit everything into your hand luggage could save you a fortune!
- Travel to and from the airport can be an issue – is there a train? How much are taxis? You don't want to get stuck paying over the odds at the airport carpark.
- Not keen on flying? There might be another option of travel, such as a train or coach, depending on where your departure destination is, of course.

Bookmark it! The Civil Aviation Authority (**www.caa.co.uk**) is an excellent resource for advice and help regarding cancellations, delays and lost luggage.

Discover more with the scenic route via train

City Break Essentials

You'll want to pack light if you are only taking a short break. Always research the climate and weather of your destination before you go, but these items will prove useful no matter what...

- **A compact raincoat**
  European weather is unpredictable!

- **Sunglasses**
  Even the coldest climates can get exceptionally bright.

- **Portable phone charger & plug adapter**
  Stay connected!

- **Camera, or the one on your phone**
  To capture those memorable moments forever.

- **A diary or notebook**
  Add all your important addresses just in case you get caught with no signal!

- **A map or guidebook**
  Again, you can't always rely on digital devices.

- **Comfortable shoes**
  You'll want to do plenty of exploring to make the most of your trip.

©Images: Getty

Accommodation
Things to consider...
- European cities offer up many options, from hostels to fancy hotels, self-catering to homestays. Some cities even offer campsites, so make sure you compare your options.
- Always ensure you think about location, transport and facilities.
- You might not spend much time in the accommodation so it could be a good place to cut costs – or maybe you're throwing the big bucks at a boutique hotel. It's up to you!
- Use compare sites but also check the official hotel websites as they could offer exclusive deals. Airbnb and HomeExchange offer house swaps, unique properties and homes away from home. For a budget base, try a hostel. Many European hostels are incredibly clean and even offer private, en-suite rooms.

Legal, money and mobile phones
Things to consider...
- Since the pandemic, some things have changed, so make sure you've done all the legal stuff that may be required for getting to your destination.
- Check on the Foreign Office site for up-to-date legal requirements and advice by country and check with your mobile provider so you understand the costs of using data abroad.
- Don't forget to order your currency ahead of time, and check for the best exchange rates online.

Make provisions ahead of time to prevent any issues

TOP TIPS

DOWNLOAD IT!
CITYMAPPER
www.citymapper.com
An essential app to help you travel across the city like a pro, available in most major cities across Europe.

Book insurance!
You might only be hopping on a flight to spend a couple of days elsewhere, but you will need to make sure you have insurance. Check out compare sites to ensure you don't pay over the odds and double-check with Defaqto (**defaqto.com**) for the provider's rating, so you can ensure you are covered by a reputable company.

Planning your time
Pick your top sights, but don't overload yourself and make sure you leave time for a stroll or having a siesta – after all, it's a holiday not a route march. Accept that you may not see everything in one weekend but try to be savvy with planning – cities are big, so clump together sights in areas so you don't end up criss-crossing all over town.

Book things ahead
Some sites require forethought – especially big ones like the Alhambra and the Colosseum, etc – so plan ahead. Booking a tour guide is a great way to get under the skin of a place and some cities have volunteer Greeters or free student guides who give you a real locals' view of the place. Also, think of your hobbies and see if there are any special tours related to them. Research local museums, tours, concerts or events in your chosen destination before you go. Do a good search online – you might find your favourite band is playing, a theatre show strikes your interest or an off-the-beaten-track haunt is only down the street from your hotel. It's easier to factor time in beforehand than try and squeeze everything in while you are already there!

Be realistic
When push comes to shove, our main piece of advice when planning a city break is to prioritise – in terms of both money and time. You probably can't afford to do everything in a city and likewise, you won't have time to see the whole lot – without getting a bit footsore and irritable anyway. Accepting that you can't do it all will lead to a more relaxing and fun city break. It also leaves the door open to a return trip in the future – why not check out the city in a different season?

"Don't overstretch yourself! Leave time for a stroll or siesta"

Useful Links

Flights
Compare flights:
Skyscanner www.skyscanner.net
Kayak www.kayak.com
Plan a stressless journey:
FlightConnections
www.flightconnections.com
Train advice:
Seat61 www.seat61.com

Accommodation
Booking.com www.booking.com
Trivago www.trivago.com
Hostel World www.hostelworld.com
Airbnb www.airbnb.com
HomeExchange www.homeexchange.com

Activities
Excursions:
Tripadvisor www.tripadvisor.com
The one-stop site to find restaurants, museums, tours and more in your chosen destination. Although be wary – reviews can be submitted by anyone, so don't rely on it for accommodation!
TourScanner www.tourscanner.com
Inspiration:
Hand Luggage Only
www.handluggageonly.co.uk
This fantastic blog is devoted to inspiring your wanderlust, packed with endless tips and advice on a wide range of destinations.
TripFiction
www.tripfiction.com
Find your next literary destination with this unique search engine designed to match you up with your favourite book's settings.

TOP CITIES

TOP CITIES

What do you want from a city escape? Are you keen to delve into a nation's history? Explore the arts scene? Take a breather in nature? Enjoy a little retail therapy? Whatever it is that you want to escape to, you are guarenteed to find it in one of these incredible European cities...

"If you are keen to soak up the customs of another culture, these cities provide endless inspiration"

TOP CITIES FOR...
Culture Seekers

From art galleries and stunning architecture to world-class museums, performing arts and flourishing music scenes. If you are keen to soak up the creative customs of another country, these cities provide endless inspiration...

Bergen

Once home to classical composers Edvard Grieg and Ole Bull, Bergen also boasts one of the world's oldest symphony orchestras, and a music scene spans from classical to electronica and extreme black metal.

Must Experience: Fantoft Stave Church, Bergenhus Fortress, KODE museums and composers' homes, Bryggen and the Hanseatic Museum, Gamlehaugen, University Museum, Old Bergen Museum, Bergen Cathedral, take the Fløibanen to Fløyen, Market Square and sample the seafood at the fish market.

Read more on page 22.

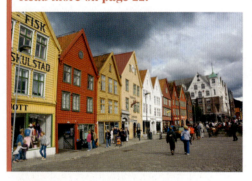

Sofia

Bulgaria's capital is set in the midst of mountains and boasts hot mineral springs, stunning parks and nearby waterfalls alongside its opulent temples, unique museums, quirky bridges and ancient ruins.

Must Experience: National Palace of Culture, Vitosha Mountain, Boyana Waterfall, Boyana Church, Museum of Illusions, Sofia Central Mineral Baths, National Historical Museum, National Art Gallery, Museum of Socialist Art, The Ethnographic Museum, National Archeological Museum, St. Alexander Nevsky Cathedral, Ivan Vazov National Theatre, grab a pastry on Pirotska street and enjoy a drink inside the National Library's bar, Once Upon a Time Biblioteka.

Read more on page 89.

Lisbon

Balancing historical charm and modern convenience, Portugal's capital city boasts a whole host of museums, stunning Baroque and Rococo architecture, as well as a vibrant street art scene.

Must Experience: Museu Nacional do Azulejo, Museu Coleção Berardo, the Museu Nacional de Arte Contemporânea do Chiado, learn about fado music at Museu do Fado (visit Barrio Alto and Alfama to catch some Fado live), Ribeira Market, a bite to eat at LX Factory. Sintra: Pena Palace and Park, Museu Nacional dos Coches, Campo Pequeno bullring, grab a drink at Pavilhão Chinês.

Read more on page 62.

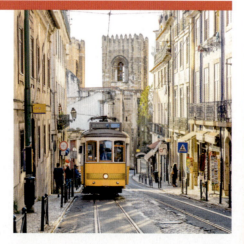

Edinburgh

Scotland's capital boasts a rich literary history from the first encyclopedia to *Harry Potter*. Plus, enjoy annual celebrations like Edinburgh Fringe, the Royal Edinburgh Military Tattoo and New Year's bash, Hogmanay.

Must Experience: Old Town and the underground city, New Town, Edinburgh Castle, Victoria Street, Scottish National Gallery & Portrait Gallery, National Museum of Scotland, the John Knox House and Scottish Storytelling Centre, Bobby the dog and the ghosts of Greyfriars Kirkyard, The Scotch Whisky Experience.

Read more on page 105.

Amsterdam

The home of Van Gogh and Rembrandt is a dream for artsy pleasure seekers. The city boasts over 51 museums, numerous art galleries, an array quirky architecture and thriving theatres.

Must Experience: Rembrandt House Museum, Van Gogh Museum, Rijksmuseum, Stedelijk Museum, the Royal Palace of Amsterdam, Sex Museum, the Amsterdam Museum, Chinatown, a canal cruise, Anne Frank House, unwind in a coffee shop, sample the wears in the largest outdoor market in Europe and pick a bloom at the Bloemenmarkt.

Read more on page 108.

TOP CITIES

TOP CITIES FOR...
History Buffs

Europe is teeming with history, from ancient ruins to heritage sites....

Tallinn

Estonia's capital features 14th-Century medieval walls surrounding its Old Town and the only surviving Gothic town hall in of northern Europe. It also boasts museums tracing every aspect of Estonian history.

Must Experience: Estonian Open Air Museum, Estonian History Museum, St Olaf's Church, Lennusadam, Viru Gate, Kiek in de Kök, Danish King's Garden, Vanalinn, Estonian Health Museum, Eesti Meremuuseum, St Catherine's Passage, Town Hall Pharmacy, Tower's Square, Tallinn City Museum, Estonian Museum of Natural History, KGB Museum, The Patarei Prison.

Read more on page 36.

Naples

The birthplace of pizza is a great place to stop off to explore Italy's heritage. From museums, catacombs and castles to the Roman ruins of Pompeii and Herculaneum – it's a history lover's dream, and you can wind down with a fresh slice of Neapolitan.

Must Experience: Pompeii, Herculaneum, Mount Vesuvius, Naples Cathedral, San Domenico Maggiore, Piazza del Plebiscito; Castel Nuovo, San Gennaro Catacombs, National Archaeological Museum, Castel dell'Ovo. Naples Underground City: the Bourbon Gallery, Cimitero delle Fontanelle, Napoli Sotterranea.

Read more on page 48.

Athens

This ancient Greek capital is one of the oldest named cities in the world and laid the foundations of western civilisation. Sitting above the hustle and bustle of modern-day Athens is the Acropolis, the remains of an ancient citadel including the legendary Parthenon, a temple devoted to the city's namesake, the goddess Athena.

Must Experience: The Acropolis: Parthenon, Herod Atticus Odeon, The Temple of Athena Nike, Old Temple of Athena, Herod Atticus Odeon and the Theatre of Dionysus, National Archaeological Museum, Panathenaic Stadium, the Acropolis Museum, Agora Museum, the Temple of Hephaestus, Temple of Olympian Zeus, Kerameikos, Benaki Museum of Greek Culture.

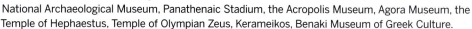

Read more on page 64.

York

The history of York is said to be the history of England, and this compact city in the north was founded by the Romans, later becoming the Viking capital of Britain. Today, it's known for its unique 14th-century cobbled streets, the shambles, the annual Jorvik festival and its magnificent 13th-Century cathedral.

Must Experience: The Jorvik Viking Centre, the shambles, York Minster Cathedral, Museum Gardens, York City Walls, National Railway Museum, Clifford's Tower, Yorkshire Museum, Betty's Tea Rooms, York's Chocolate Story, York Castle Museum, Merchant Adventurers' Hall, Barley Hall, The Bar Convent Living Heritage Centre, Dick Turpin's grave, a glass of mead at Valhalla bar.

Read more on page 98.

Matera

Famed for the Sassi di Matera, complex cave dwellings that are thought to date back as far as the Palaeolithic era. This prehistoric troglodyte settlement is generally considered the oldest continuously inhabited human settlement in Italy and perhaps in the world. The general population was evacuated in 1952, due to rampant poverty and disease, but today you can enjoy a variety of hotels, museums and restaurants situated within the caves.

Must Experience: Streets of the Sassi, Chiesa di Santa Maria di Idris, Convento di Sant'Agostino, San Pietro Caveoso, San Pietro Barisano, Matera Cathedral, MUSMA, Crypt of Original Sin (Cripta del Peccato Originale), Parco delle Chiese Rupestri di Matera, Museum of Applied Arts (La Casa di Ortega), Palace of the Seat (Palazzo del Sedile).

Read more on page 49.

©Images: Getty

TOP CITIES FOR...
Nature Lovers

Are you looking for a getaway that is immersed in nature but has the convenience of being in a city? Look no further than these five cities that will provide the best of both worlds.

Reykjavik

Iceland's capital is teeming with natural wonders. It's easy to see why the Vikings regarded the country the land of the gods thanks to its apocalyptic mix of volcanoes, glaciers, haunting rock formations, eutrophic lakes, waterfalls and black sand beaches.

Must Experience: Blue Lagoon geothermal spa, The Golden Circle (Thingvellir National Park, Gullfoss waterfall and Geysir geothermal area), Bruarfoss waterfall, the northern lights at Aurora Reykjavik, the Perlan Museum of Icelandic Natural Wonders, go whale watching, Mount Esja, Videy Island, the Volcano House, Reykjavik Maritime Museum.

Read more on page 34.

Tromso

The Paris Of The North, Tromsø, is perhaps as close as you can get to the wilderness while maintaining a city setting. Wildlife and nature is heavily woven into the fabric of this gateway to the arctic – as is the ability to unwind with a pint!

Must Experience: Tromso fjord cruise, Northern lights tour (in winter), dog sledding, whale watching, reindeer sledding and feeding, the Arctic Cathedral, Polaria Arctic Experience Centre and Aquarium, The Polar Museum, Tromsø Museum, Fløya mountain, watch the midnight sun (in summer), Tromsø Wilderness Center on Kvaloya, Tromsø Arctic-Alpine Botanical Garden, fishing in Hella, Bukta beach.

Read more on page 24.

Dubrovnik

The 'pearl of the Adriatic' Dubrovnik, like much of Croatia, is both rich in history and culture and stunning scenery. Situated between Mount Srdj and the Adriatic sea, its lavish beaches attract flocks of tourists for good reason.

Must Experience: Take a cable car to Mount Srđ, the island of Lokrum, Krka National Park and witness the Skradinski Buk waterfalls, Trsteno Renaissance Garden, Odysseus' Cave at Mljet National Park, Blue Cave, Elafiti Islands, Korcula Islands, Fort Lovrijenac and Sulic beach, sea kayaking, relax on Banje beach or the smaller Sveti Jakov where you can then hike to Park Orsula, Trsteno Arboretum botanical gardens.

Read more on page 88.

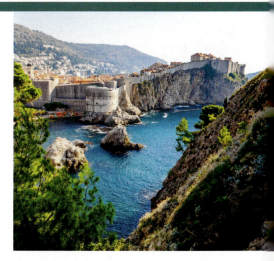

Kotor

Located within a picturesque bay surrounded by mountains, Kotor offers an exceptional mixture of history and nature. Montenegro's historic fortress city is a stone's throw away from the country's national parks and heritage sites.

Must Experience: Kotor Cats Museum, relax on Kotor beach, hike to Saint John's Fortress via the Ladder of Kotor, hike the historical slopes of the Lovćen mountain, visit the old city walls, Kotor Maritime Museum, walk the city walls, take a dip in the Blue Cave, kayak or paddle board the bay of Kotor, white water rafting in the Tara canyon.

Read more on page 83.

Bern

Switzerland's capital is a stone's throw away from the Alps, offers wild swimming, roses, chocolates and a park full of bears alongside its historic well-preserved Medieval city centre.

Must Experience: Bärengraben (the bear pit), Rosengarten (Rose Garden Park), Gurten mountain, explore Emmental valley, consider a helicopter tour of the Alps, visit one of the area's nature parks (Gantrisch, Diemtigtal or Chasseral), take a dip in the river Aare, Swiss Alpine Museum, check out ski resort Gstaad (hike in summer, ski in winter) and bathe in the Alp turnels to unwind, stargaze at Uecht, follow the Witch's Trail around Schwarzsee's mountain lake, take the train to the 'top of Europe': Jungfraujoch.

Read more on page 115.

TOP CITIES FOR...
Foodies

They say the way to someone's heart is through their belly. If that's the case, you will fall head over heels for these delicious destinations...

Bologna

Naturally, if you are a fan of food, Italy is a fantastic choice for a meal-focused trip. The city of Bologna is famed for its rich red Bolognese spaghetti sauce but that's not the only tasty dish the city has to offer as Italy's gastronomical capital.

Must Experience: Food stores Paolo Atti & Figli and A.F. Tamburini on Via Caprarie, Quadrilatero market, Mercato di Mezzo, Tamburini cafe, Salumeria Simoni, sip some wine at Bologna's oldest bar Osteria del Sole, treat yourself to a chocolate or two at Caffe Zanarini, Palazzo della Mercanzia (where the original recipe and exact measurements for tortellini is held), Le Sfogline, Mercato delle Erbe under-cover market.

Read more on page 45.

Copenhagen

Sample Scandi dishes in Denmark's fairytale city. The home of the Little Mermaid has made waves across the culinary world thanks to one particular restaurant, Noma, which won the title of World's Best Restaurant from 2010-2014 and 2021, thanks to its 'New Nordic' cuisine.

Must Experience: Noma, ex-Noma chef restaurants Amass, 108 and Sanchez, sample sweet treats at Mirabelle, a beer-focused dining experience at Restaurant Barr (Noma's former haunt), eat Smørrebrød at Aamanns 1921, Alchemist, Torvehallerne food hall, indulge in an authentic Danish dinner at Schønnemann, grab porridge for breakfast at Grød, a craft beer at Mikkeller Bar and some vino at Den Vandrette.

Read more on page 32.

Porto

World-famous thanks to Port wine, Portugal's port city is a foodie hotspot for indulging in everything from speciality sandwiches and cheese to fish and fine dining.

Must Experience: A Francesinha (a decadent cheese and meat sandwich that's impossible to eat with your hands) at Cafe Santiago, sip fortified wine at the port lodges in Vila Nova de Gaia, Casa de Chá da Boa Nova, the Yeatman, Tia Tia's natural wines, dine on the beach at Chez Maurice, sample the flavours of Portugal at Restaurante Dona Maria, Amaral Cheese Factory.

Read more on page 61.

TOP CITIES

San Sebastián

This scenic Spanish Basque coastal city boasts golden beaches, luscious hillsides and the second most Michelin stars per capita in the whole world (behind only Kyoto, Japan) and is home to the Basque answer to tapas: the pintxo.

Must Experience: The Michelin three-star awarded restaurants: Akelarre, Arzak and Martín Berasategui – make sure you try bacalao pil pil (a form of salt cod cooked in olive oil), kokotxas (stew made with cod or hake cheeks), Txuleta beef and pastel vasco pastry – the two-Michelin-star Mugaritz, the San Martín and La Bretxa food markets, join a pintxo tour.

Read more on page 58.

Lyon

Home to 17 Michelin-starred restaurants, Lyon has enjoyed the title 'the Gastronomic Capital of the World' since 1935. The city entered the culinary map thanks to the Mothers of Lyon back in the 19th century and has continued to enjoy such foodie fame due to the 'Chef of the Century', the late Paul Bocuse.

Must Experience: Les Halles de Lyon Paul Bocuse market, an authentic bouchon (try Daniel et Denise Créqui, Le Garet, Cafe des Federations), sample sabodet at Reynon, Maison Troisgros, try the Pot-au-Feu and Lièvre à la Royale (wild hare stew) at Paul Bocuse, outdoor markets Marché de la Croix-Rousse and Marché Saint-Antoine, satiate your sweet tooth with coussins de Lyon.

Read more on page 126.

©Images: Getty

TOP CITIES FOR...

If you enjoy acquiring mementos from your travels, look no further than these four cities – from upmarket boutiques to bartering flea markets, you are sure to find something unique.

Shopaholics

Stockholm

Scandinavians are infamously effortlessly chic. Renowned for their minimalism, Swedish design has gone global thanks to the likes of Ikea and H&M, and the country's capital is a hot spot for ethical skincare, fashion and homeware.

Must Experience: Drottninggatan, Hornsgatan (for art, vintage and second-hand wares), MOOD Stockholm, Hötorget flea market, Designtorget for Swedish-made pieces, Hornstulls Strand flea market, the antique stores of Vasastan, Nordiska Kompaniet department store, Stora Nygatan, Gamla Stan, explore the side streets of Götgatsbacken, SoFo (Lisa Larsson, Acne Studio and Kult & Design on Bondegatan), Sturegallerian, Grandpa.

Read more on page 26.

Barcelona

The Catalonia capital is one of the top ten global fashion capitals in the world. Pick from one of its eight shopping areas and you could enjoy scouring its stunning Art Nouveau streets of Barcelona's Golden Mile, Paseo de Gràcia, for the latest in luxury fashion. Search for vintage gems, alt fashion and records on Calle Tallers, or sample local specialities with the Spanish seal of excellence and hand-crafted items at Sant Antoni Market.

Must Experience: Paseo de Gràcia, La Diagona, traditional shops in the Gothic Quarter, local wears in Sant Antoni, boho-chic boutiques in El Born, La Rambla and La Boquería Market, alternative clothing, vintage and music stores in El Raval.

Read more on page 54.

Florence

While this beautiful Tuscan capital is renowned for its wealth, it is also a great place to pick up bargains. The compact city can be scoured by foot and is full of traditional artisans selling quality products for low prices, from bespoke, handmade real leather goods to tailored clothing and stunning jewellery.

Must Experience: Santo Spirito and Santa Croce – don't miss AquaFlor Firenze for exquisite perfumes – Il Torchio traditional bookbinders, the Officina Profumo-Farmaceutica di Santa Maria Novella for a spot of self-care, Madova bespoke gloves, Atelier Scriptorium Firenze to resurrect the now lost tradition of letter-writing on custom stationary, San Lorenzo outdoor leather market.

Read more on page 44.

Istanbul

If you prefer to shop for unique items full of cultural creativity, Istanbul is a shopper's delight. Stunning Persian carpets, Byzantine-style jewellery, Ottoman antiques, hand-made ceramics and more are on offer at the world famous Grand Bazaar. You can even grab an authentic belly dancing costume and spices to inject some exotic flavour into your next dishes. The sprawling streets of Galata offer chic boutiques and a bird's eye view of the whole city from the it's historic tower.

Must Experience: Grand Bazaar, Serdar-ı Ekrem Street, Ali Muhiddin Hacı Bekir, the quirky shops of Balat, Istiklal Caddesi, Kurukahveci Mehmet Efendi for coffee, shop vintage wears in Çukurcuma, for luxury brands check out Nışantası district.

Read more on page 90.

Tip!

If you live outside the EU and are visiting an EU country or vice versa, you may be eligible for a VAT refund. There may be a minimum spend, just check the city's local tourist information and don't forget to request a tax-free form when you make your purchase if required.

TOP CITIES

TOP CITIES FOR...

Nightlife

Whether you are plotting a stag, planning a hen, or just enjoy going wild on the weekend, these cities are hotspots for late night fun...

Budapest

Budapest is famous for its ruin bars – old dilapidated Communist-era buildings that have seen new life as late-night boozers. Visit in the summer and the Hungarian capital will bring your inner beast out with their spa parties – often held on a full moon.

Must Experience: Budapest's old Jewish quarter, Budapest's original ruin bar Szimpla Kert, Neverland, Doboz, Ötkert, neo speakeasy Boutiq'Bar, start the night on Gozsdu Passage for a bite and end it with karaoke, the Sparty at Szechenyi Baths, Racskert, Fogas Ház, Gödör.

Read more on page 79.

Berlin

Berlin's clubbing scene is off the hook. If you are on the lookout for nonstop nightlife, Germany's legendary capital is the city that never sleeps, check out everything from techno raves and hip-hop clubs to cabaret shows, laid-back bars and traditional beer gardens.

Must Experience: Berlin's oldest biergarten the Prater Biergarten, the raver's 'church' Berghain, Ritter Butzke, Clärchens Ballhaus for Gatsby vibes, the hedonistic KitKat, Kreuzberg, Tresor, Wilde Renate, Klunkerkranich, take a toilet selfie in Geist im Glas.

Read more on page 120.

Riga

The capital of Latvia is a culture-seeker's paradise full of history and tradition, but it is also home to some of Europe's best nightlife. Old Town is the city's historic hub, but also its party central. Its bars and clubs are all within walking distance, meaning it's ideal if you are planning to get a little wobbly.

Must Experience: Handle medieval weaponry with a pint in hand at the Armoury Bar, Depo, Cynic Bar, Skyline Bar, La Rocca, Folkklubs ALA Pagrabs subterranean bar, a tipple of black balsam at Black Magic, time travel to the Soviet 1970s at Gauja, Taka for craft beer, rockers will love the biker atmosphere of Roks Cepure or the underground Riga Rock Cafe.

Read more on page 37.

Prague

The Czech capital caters to every kind of partier, whoever you are, you're guaranteed to have a blast. It's also home to Europe's largest club, Karlovy Lázně, the five-storey venue is a hotspot for clubbers.

Must Experience: Karlovy Lázně, MeetFactory for a little bit of everything, rockers check out Hells Bells Rockin' Pub and Harley's, Futurum for never-ending fun, Malkovich, Black Angel's, get comfy at BED, Hemingway Bar, Bugsy's, the Cross Club bar, Chapeau Rouge, a pint of Czech beer at Beer Point.

Read more on page 74.

Dublin

If you are a fan of a good old-fashioned pub, look no further than the Irish capital. With over 750 of them, you'd be hard-pressed not to find one you love – and don't forget to order a jar of Guinness.

Must Experience: The Temple Bar Pub, Porterhouse Temple Bar, Bad Bobs, Vintage Cocktail Club, The Old Storehouse, The Cauldron, The Brazen Head, Copper Faced Jacks, Pygmalion, Tramline, Opium Club, Dicey's Garden, the Mexican-themed Xico.

Read more on page 103.

INTRO

20 **NORTH**
Tromsø - page 22

38 **SOUTH**
Seville - page 51

68 **EAST & CENTRAL**
Dubrovnik - page 86

92 **WEST**
Zurich - page 112

GEORGIA
TURKEY

NORTH

22 Bergen
24 Tromso
25 Oslo
26 Stockholm
28 Gothenburg
29 Turku
30 Helsinki
32 Copenhagen
33 Aarhus
34 Reyjavik
35 Vilnus
36 Tallinn
37 Riga

BERGEN

IF YOU'RE PINING FOR THE FJORDS, NORWAY'S FORMER CAPITAL IS THE PLACE FOR YOU

Bryggen's quaint wooden houses are a perfect backdrop to the serene harbour waters

Essential information

There is an average of 200 days of rain per year in Bergen — so don't forget your coat!

Best time to visit Between April and September (as some attractions close during winter)

Currency kr · Norwegian Krone

Time zone UTC+1

NORTH

Bergen fish market is always bustling with some of the freshest catches the North Sea has to offer

FISH FOOD

Inevitably, due to its location, one of Bergen's major trades was fish. The fish market has stood on the wharf since 1276 and should certainly form part of your trip there, if you can cope with the whiff. Bergen's rich history in the fish trade has led to a vast appreciation of the culinary arts and this led to it being named as a UNESCO City of Gastronomy. You won't have to walk far to find the delicious aromas of fish soup, fish cakes or persetorsk (steamed cod) wafting out from one of the many restaurants on the wharf and in the town. For seafood lovers, Bergen is a little slice of heaven in a big slice of fish pie.

"Bergen is the city that has it all. Scenery, culture, history, food, nightlife..."

Given that Norway is known as the Land of the Fjords, boasting over one thousand of the glacier-carved waterways, to be known as the country's Heart of the Fjords is a prestigious title indeed. That honour falls to Bergen, the second-largest city in Norway, found on the south-west coast overlooking the North Sea. Bergen is situated between Hardangerfjord and the Sognefjord, Norway's two largest fjords, so you can see how it gets its nickname. If you're interested in visiting these stunning, enormous natural canals, created over thousands of years at a literal glacial pace, then Bergen is absolutely the place to visit. It acts as the start or end point of many a fjord cruise, but is so much more than just a landing ground.

Bergen is packed with over 750 years' worth of history, culture, art, food and music. Back in the 12th and 13th centuries, Bergen was the nation's capital and you can understand why. It was the gateway to mainland Europe and the rest of the world, perfectly placed to send and receive ships laden with goods for trade. The wharf on which thousands of deals were struck for materials, food, drink and precious artefacts is no longer a trade port, but is now a piece of living history, lined with shops, galleries, restaurants and museums, selling materials, food, drink and precious artefacts. Some things never change. Bryggen is listed as a UNESCO World Heritage Site and still retains many of its ancient features, having been rebuilt in the traditional style each time fire caught hold of its picturesque, if flammable, wooden houses. A nod to Bergen's seafaring past can be found in the monument in Torgallmenningen Square, a pretty area surrounded by shops and cafes.

However, Bergen is far from a dusty, fusty former port that still clings onto its industrial past. It has a vibrant, exciting art scene that has a little something for everyone. KODE is one of the largest art, design and music museums in the Nordic countries and offers tourists a wonderful glimpse into the Nordic way of life. It houses many works of art by Norwegian artist Edvard Munch, and although his most famous work, The Scream, lives in Oslo, there is plenty to enjoy. Troldhaugen, the former home of composer Edvard Grieg, is a living museum dedicated to one of Bergen's most famous residents. Sticking to the theme of music, Bergen Philharmonic Orchestra is one of the oldest in the world, so a trip to the concert hall is worth it, even if you can't stay for a concerto. And for those of you who prefer their art a little more street, a little more modern, Skostredeet, one of Bergen's best shopping areas, is decorated with ever-changing graffiti art.

If that is a little too 21st century for you, then Bergen is teeming with relics of its former life as Norway's gateway to Europe. Not all visitors to Norway's shores were friendly traders, as shown by the presence of Bergenhaus Fortress, a mostly ruined construction which still retains parts from the 1240s. Armed with a good pair of walking boots, trekking the Fortress trail offers wonderful views of the city and sea, while the cannons get fired on certain national holidays. St Mary's Church is on the northern part of Bryggen and offers you a step even further back in time, having been built in the 12th century, and is a beautiful example of Romanesque architecture. To the north of Bergen is the charming and unique Old Bergen Museum. However, this isn't your standard, stuffy collection of old pictures, rather a living, breathing village made up of around 50 reconstructed houses from the 18th, 19th and 20th centuries. You can explore the houses, chill in the park and chat to the actors playing the roles of lords and servants learning everything about life in the Bergen of old.

Bergen's man-made sights are a real treat, but the main course has to be its unbelievably picturesque scenery. As well as being the Heart of the Fjords, Bergen is also known as the City Between Seven Mountains, nestled within soaring natural skyscrapers. To get an impressive aerial view, take the Floibanen funicular up Floyen mountain, 320 metres (1050 feet) above sea level. Or, if that's not high enough for you, Ulkriken cable car more than doubles that, whizzing you 643 metres (2100 feet) above sea level to a vantage point on Ulkriken Mountain. From there you can enjoy staggering vistas of the city and countryside, all while breathing in the gorgeous mountain air. You can also experience the mountains by rail. Take the Bergen railway, cutting through the heart of the mountains to Oslo, or stop off in Flam and hop on the Flam Railway — known as one of the world's most beautiful train routes — to take in the breathtaking unspoiled scenery.

With all your sightseeing ticked off, and if you have enough energy in your legs, Bergen has a thriving nightlife scene, due to its relatively large student population. There is a healthy array of restaurants, bars and clubs to keep you entertained late into the night.

Bergen really is the city that has it all. Scenery, culture, history, sights, food, nightlife... If you love all of the finer things in life, then the Heart of the Fjords will truly steal yours.

Useful sites

en.visitbergen.com
visitnorway.com/places-to-go/fjord-norway/bergen
vy.no/en/traffic-and-routes/stations-and-network-maps/the-bergen-line

The funicular and cable cars that take you up Bergen's mountains are almost as enjoyable as the views

TROMSØ

THIS BUZZING ARCTIC METROPOLIS HAS MORE TO OFFER THAN JUST CHASING THE NORTHERN LIGHTS

The eye-catching Arctic Cathedral dominates the Tromsø skyline

Since its official founding in the late-18th century, Norway's northern city of Tromsø has surprised and enticed visitors with its rich culture and historic heritage. Dubbed the 'Paris of the North', Tromsø has much more to offer tourists than just the northern lights – although many who visit eagerly watch the skies in the hope of catching the elusive light display.

To aid intrepid aurora-chasers, there are several tour operators based in the city centre, offering everything from large-group bus tours to private excursions tailored to your specification. Tours don't come cheap, though – starting at around £87 ($110), prices increase the smaller your group gets.

However, even a bog-standard bus tour will give you up to six hours of light chasing, taking you to several picturesque locations and providing you with a guide who'll talk you through how to capture the aurora on your camera. As a gesture of goodwill, most reputable operators will offer you a second tour for free if the lights don't make an appearance on your first.

It's not just aurora tours on offer, however. Husky sledding trips are available to tourists during the snow season, and whale-watching cruises set sail from the harbour daily. Both are once-in-a-lifetime experiences, and naturally come with a price tag to match.

On the more affordable end of the spectrum, outdoorsy sorts will relish the city's local viewing platform located on the plateau of Mount Storsteinen. Reached either by walking or taking the four-minute Fjellheisen cable car (approximately £20/$25 for an adult return), visitors can witness panoramic views over the city. It's also a popular spot for summer tourists wishing to experience the midnight Sun in all its glory, or those winter visitors seeking a closer northern lights encounter.

For those searching for the city's celebrated culture, head to the museums and galleries to learn more about Tromsø's Sami and Norse heritage. The local art gallery, the Nordnorsk Kunstmuseum, is home to a range of art, from paintings by popular Norwegian artist Edvard Munch, to creations by the world-famous British artist David Hockney.

Like everything else, food and drink doesn't come cheap in Tromsø. For those willing to splurge, Mathallen serves traditional cuisine in a cosy environment. However, if you're looking for something a little more affordable, Tromsø has several hole-in-the-wall-type setups offering more budget-friendly food, including Raketten, a kiosk on the main high street, Storgata. Huken Pub has proven popular with tourists and locals alike, serving food as well as drinks – be aware that alcohol is priced at a premium in Tromsø. Speak to staff at your hotel to find out their affordable recommendations, too.

Essential information

Prepare for your visit – while temperatures regularly drop to lows of -6°C (21°F) in winter, it's the lack of sunlight that can be hardest to acclimatise to.

Best time to visit September to March (the best time to catch the northern lights)

Currency kr · Norwegian Krone

Time zone UTC+1

Useful sites

www.visittromso.no/en

norway.nordicvisitor.com/travel-guide/attractions/north-norway/

Hallo!

NORTH

OSLO

EXPLORE THIS NORTHERN CAPITAL'S MASTERY OF BOTH NATURAL BEAUTY AND ARCHITECTURAL GRANDEUR

Whether you're testing your resolve in its harsh winters or prefer to make the most of the Norwegian capital while the Sun still shines, Oslo is a city that's ready and able to provide whatever the weather. While many may travel looking for a blanket of the white stuff to hurl themselves down a mountain, Oslo is just as suitable for summer trips, too. You may want to take a boat trip out on the fjords, for example, and the chance to glimpse a dolphin cresting the surface is likely not worth combating the bitter winds in winter.

In fact, you'll be thankful for Norway's long summer days – where the Sun doesn't really set until midnight – because when it comes to exploring Oslo's natural environments, there's just too much to fit in. Neighbouring hikes, island hopping across the fjord, meandering the Akerselva river that cuts through the city; Norway's serene natural environment takes centrestage in Oslo. The open-air museum at Ekebergparken is particularly compelling in the warmer months, with numerous sculptures dotted across the hilltop that overlooks the fjord below. And if it's sculptures you're looking for, Oslo is home to the world's largest sculpture park in Frogner Park, and the Vigeland installation within, with more than 200 intricate bronze and granite statues created by Gustav Vigeland.

But don't overlook Oslo when it dons its winter gown, either. Not only do the colder temperatures – which are still mild by inland Norwegian standards – mean that the streets aren't quite as crammed with tourists, but there's a delicate beauty to the city when it's coated in a layer of the white stuff. The varied and eclectic contemporary architecture of Oslo is certainly one of the major reasons to explore the city, but it's hard not to be captivated when those straight edges of steel and glass are softened by snow. The renovated docklands of Sørenga is the prime spot for this, offering panoramic views of the Oslo skyline, waterside restaurants and a pleasant stroll past the Opera House – the most prominent example of modern architecture in the city.

Oslo doesn't close up shop in the winter, either. Numerous ice rinks appear throughout the city, the huge ski jump and museum at Holmenkollen becomes a worthwhile destination, and a nearby sledding track all make for unique activities that many other cities can't provide. If you're feeling really brave, you could even test your resolve against the Scandinavians and try hopping directly from a sauna into the icy cold waters surrounding the city. While Oslo may be able to cater for the warmth, the mark it'll leave if you visit in the winter will be indelible.

Useful sites
www.oslo.com
www.visitnorway.com/places-to-go/eastern-norway/oslo
www.salted.no/sauna

Essential information

Oslo can be expensive, but there are lots of free events and attractions available.

Best time to visit June to July (for the mild weather and midnight Sun) or winter (for lower room rates and winter activities)

Currency kr · Norwegian Krone

Time zone UTC+1

Touring the islands on Oslofjord is a pleasant day trip

"Oslo is a city that's able to provide whatever the weather"

Akershus Fortress is a medieval castle that's been used as a military base and prison in the past

STOCKHOLM
DISCOVER WHY SWEDEN'S BEAUTIFUL CAPITAL IS A CITY OF CONTRASTS

Known as the "world's smallest big city" or "biggest town", Stockholm isn't one of the bigger cities in Europe, but it is a major player in terms of what it has to offer. The capital is a city of contrasts. You can explore it on land or from the water, take in its rich history or modern art and discover its urban or green spaces. There's something for everyone, which makes it ideal for a European city break.

At 6,519 km² (2,517 sq mi) Sweden's capital isn't exactly small, but, despite its size, it is still walkable. Start your tour of the city on foot by wandering through the cobbled, winding streets of the old town (Gamla Stan). Dating back to 1252, this charming area is one of Europe's most well preserved medieval city centres. As well as the iconic coloured houses of Stortoget Square, here you'll find the city's oldest street, Köpmangatan, and its smallest street, Mårten Trotzigs gränd at 90cm (35in) wide (stand in the alleyway and you can touch either side). Shop for a souvenir at Västergatan Street before visiting other gems in the heart of the city, whether it be the baroque Royal Palace to see the changing of the guards, the Riksdag (Swedish Parliament), Storkyrkan (Stockholm Cathedral), Hallwyl Museum (renaissance home to aristocrats Walther von Hallwyl and his wife Wilhelmina) or the Nobel Prize Museum.

From the old town, head south to the new city, the young and hip Södermalm. Once voted one of the coolest neighbourhoods in the world by Vogue, Söder has a laidback, creative vibe. Go check out the contemporary photography exhibitions at Fotografiska, eat, drink or go clubbing in SoFo or take a walk along clifftop path Monteliusvägen at sunset for one of the best views of the city. The neighbourhood also has Hornstull Marknad, a flea market with tasty street food and one of the city centre's biggest parks, Tantoludens.

If you're after green space, you'll want to visit Djurgården Island, which is part of Stockholm's

Essential information

🇸🇪 The city can be expensive, but there's plenty of free museums and if you check the SL website, some ferries are free at certain times too.

Best time to visit May to September for the best weather

Currency kr · Swedish Krona

Time zone UTC+1

Gamla Stan is known for its colourful houses

NORTH

Stadion metro station exhibits incredible rainbow artwork

Drottningholm Palace is just 50 minutes away from the centre of Stockholm

A ROYAL DAY TRIP

You're spoiled for choice when it comes to ideas for day trips from Stockholm, but Drottningholm Palace ranks highly on the list. Just 50 minutes away lies the official residence of the king and queen of Sweden, Drottningholm Palace. The Versailles-inspired palace is a UNESCO World Heritage site and one of the best preserved Swedish castles from the 17th century.

Take a cruise along Lake Mälaren. Admire the court theatre, the baroque gardens, the Chinese Pavillion and the beautiful architecture and interiors of the palace itself. Hope on a ferry from the City Hall Quay (a chance to see one of the city's other famous landmarks) and enjoy a cruise along Lake Mälaren to Lovön island that sits on the archipelago.

Other day trips include visits to the oldest university at Uppsala, Sweden's oldest town Sigtuna and the island of Sandham.

Cardamom buns make the perfect sweet treat for fika

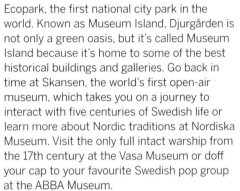

Ecopark, the first national city park in the world. Known as Museum Island, Djurgården is not only a green oasis, but it's called Museum Island because it's home to some of the best historical buildings and galleries. Go back in time at Skansen, the world's first open-air museum, which takes you on a journey to interact with five centuries of Swedish life or learn more about Nordic traditions at Nordiska Museum. Visit the only full intact warship from the 17th century at the Vasa Museum or doff your cap to your favourite Swedish pop group at the ABBA Museum.

History buffs are sorted in this retro-rich metropolis, but for those with more modern tastes there's plenty to see too. As well as beautiful old architecture, the city is known for its minimalist designs and buildings. The Globe, an entertainment area in the shape of a giant sphere, is just one example of modern architecture. Opened in 1989, the Globe is the largest spherical building in the world, with a diameter of 110m (361ft). The Stockholm Waterfront is another example of modern architecture that stands out against the city's skyline with its steel spikes.

And there's plenty to see in terms of modern art too. The Moderna Musset, based on the island of Skeppsholmen, is the leasing museum for contemporary art in Sweden. Or if you're after something a bit more unique, grab a Stockholm travelcard and go underground to see the world's longest art exhibit in the city's subway system. Over 90 metro stations showcase incredible modern artwork. Fashion lovers should explore Norrmalm & Östermalm north of Gamla Stan for the city's best shopping. Try the Strandvägen boulevard if you're after something more high-end.

Once you've done a bit of walking, you'll want to see the city from the water. Known as the "Venice of the North" or the "beauty on the water", Stockholm is positioned where Sweden's third largest lake, Lake Mälaren, meets the Baltic Sea so you can't go far without seeing water and the views are stunning. Stockholm is made up of 14 islands and each of them has something to offer the intrigued traveller, no matter how small. Take a boat tour, rent a kayak or canoe to explore the canals and waterways that interconnect them or hop on a steamer boat for a day trip to see the Stockholm archipelago, Skärgård, a group of 30,000 islands 20 minutes away.

Have you worked up an appetite yet? There are even contrasts in the flavours of the food in Stockholm. Try savoury meatballs or fried herring with a tart lingonberry sauce or jam. And don't forget fika, a meet-up for coffee and a pastry, typically a kanelbullar or cardamom bun, which contrast a sweet crunch on the outside with a spiced, fluffy inside.

And finally what bigger contrast is there than the weather between summer and winter? Stockholm in the summer allows a visitor to bask in 18+ hours of sunshine per day, while during the winter the six hours of sunlight increases the chances of seeing the Northern Lights. Whether it's shimmering in the summer sun or covered in snow, we can almost guarantee that you'll fall in love with every aspect of this city of contrasts.

Useful sites
gocity.com/stockholm/en-us
sl.se/en/in-english/fares--tickets/
www.stromma.com/

Hallå!

The Älvsborgsbron, a suspension bridge connecting the island of Hisingen with the mainland

GOTHENBURG

SMALLER THAN STOCKHOLM BUT LARGER THAN LIFE, THE WEST COAST OF SWEDEN SINGS

Gothenburg, the second-largest city in Sweden, is an eclectic mix of serenity, culture, excitement and the unusual. Take the pacifier tree in Slottsskogen park – a tree hung with pacifiers, offered as gifts to help children part with them, it makes for a both touching and amusing sight. Slottsskogen offers a lot more besides – check out the zoo, the lakes and woodland of the 137-hectare park itself, and the Gothenburg Natural History Museum, where you can not only see the world's only mounted blue whale but, on special occasions, visit a lounge inside its belly. All of this is free to enter.

If you crave relaxation, don't miss the free sauna, located in Jubileumsparken in Frihamnen, which reopens after renovation in summer 2023. If, however, you're in search of peace away from the city, venture out into the archipelago, either for a day trip or an overnight stop on one of the many islands. Visit Hönö for a seal safari, Styrsö for the scenic path up to Stora Rös, offering a panoramic view of the islands from the top, Brännö for the Thursday-night summer dances on the jetty, neighbouring Galterö for the nature reserve, or Donsö for the August Hamnfest, where vendors fill in the distinctive red fisherman's huts while water games and live music electrify the harbour. All ferries run regularly year-round and are part of the city's public transport system – you can get a 24-hour pass for £9 ($11) or a 72-hour pass for £18 ($22).

For a bit more excitement, visit in August for the eclectic, meat-free Way Out West festival, with 2022 headliners such as Tame Impala and Nick Cave and the Bad Seeds. One-day tickets are generally around £129 ($155), with a three-day pass around £257 ($311). For a cheaper, year-round adrenaline rush, opt for Liseberg. The biggest amusement park in Scandinavia, it boasts rollercoasters, the steampunk-esque Luna Park and seasonal events such as haunted houses for Hallowe'en and a charming, rustic Christmas market. Currently, the all-in-one admission and rides bundle is £20-£28 ($24-$34) and must be pre-booked.

Finally, who can visit Sweden without being drawn to the food? When it comes to sampling local delicacies, look no further than Saluhallen, the largest indoor market in the city. Open every day except Sunday, try traditional kavring from Steinbrenner & Nyberg, Danish smörrebröd from Oscar & den Lille, or one of the 300 types of cheese from Hilda Nilsson Ost. From here, stroll through the Kungsparken, magnificent in all seasons, to Palmhuset, a tropical jungle of a greenhouse in the horticultural gardens – all free to enter.

If you still have the time and energy, explore Haga, the oldest part of Gothenburg. Wander the cobbled streets winding through traditional wooden buildings, peruse the small shops, and take fika in a tiny cafe. To experience the tradition like a local, visit in the winter and wrap up in a blanket, which many cafes provide, to make your trip feel like home.

Useful sites
www.goteborg.com/en
www.vasttrafik.se/en
www.storasaluhallen.se

Essential information

Avoid the expensive, touristy Avenyn boulevard for drinking and dining; instead, pay a visit to Järntorget and Andra långgatan.

Best time to visit June to September (particularly for seeing the archipelago)

Currency kr · Swedish krona

Time zone UTC+1

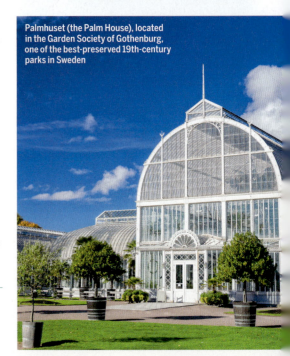

Palmhuset (the Palm House), located in the Garden Society of Gothenburg, one of the best-preserved 19th-century parks in Sweden

NORTH

TURKU

AN AGE-OLD RIVER SEPARATES THIS FINNISH CITY'S MIX OF OLD AND NEW

Essential information

Be sure to bring decent thermals if you're travelling in winter – underestimate a Scandinavian winter at your peril!

Best time to visit Spring, for the snowmelt and blooms, or June to August if you like warmer weather

Currency € · Euro

Time zone UTC+2

How to get there Board the train from the Finnish capital, Helsinki – the journey takes two hours. The bus takes the same amount of time

With a surge in flights announced by Air Baltic to this enchanting Finnish region, it's no wonder avid travellers are keen to drive tourism to Turku. Located on the southwest coast of Finland, about two hours from Helsinki by bus or train, Turku was founded in the 13th century and was in fact the Finnish capital until Russia took over the land in the early 1800s. This gives the city a rich mix of communist and European architecture, one of its main selling points.

The River Aura's waterside path is the perfect way to get to know the city by foot, as it offers unparalleled snapshots of the remarkable buildings along the route. The Aura is typically scattered with canal boats and tour operators offering reasonable prices for trips up and down its frigid waters.

In fact, the river itself plays a major role in city life. The local custom in Turku is to say that something is found 'on this side of the river' or 'the other side of the river'. This is because Turku is a city split into old and new. The older side features the city's grand Cathedral and Old Great Square, whereas the so-called new side features a modern city centre, market square and shopping malls.

Foodies will be delighted with the plethora of cafes and restaurants along the Aura's banks. Each serves real authentic Finnish cuisine, such as cinnamon rolls and Karelian pasties, as well as the more daring pickled herrings, sautéed reindeer and salty liquorice. Fish is as popular as meat in Finland, given the location of the nation near the Baltic Sea. Kalakukko is a regional delicacy – a fish pie made from rye bread, made moist by the bread soaking in the bones of the fish, giving it exquisite flavours.

Turku Cathedral is a stunning sight known locally as the Mother Church of the Evangelical Lutheran Church of Finland. Its spectacular name suits the building, which at summertime boasts an array of colourful tulips at its door, while in winter the trees that enclose the church are lit up to make it look all the more Christmassy. The cathedral is widely considered to be Finland's most valuable historical monument, and inside it features sculptures of saints as well as fine silverware from the Middle Ages.

Active folks can partake in a more adventurous side to Finnish culture. Ice swimming may sound terrifying but it gives those brave enough the chance to see Turku's beautiful forests and lakes on the outskirts of the city. Alternatively, there are many steamy saunas scattered around the city, for those less fond of the freezing temperatures.

Useful sites
visitturku.fi/en
visitfinland.com/article/turku
turku.fi

"The River Aura's waterside path is the perfect way to get to know the city"

HELSINKI

DISCOVER WHY FINLAND'S CAPITAL IS KNOWN AS THE "PEARL OF THE BALTIC"

While it's not as popular as other Scandinavian cities such as Stockholm and Copenhagen, Helsinki is known as the "daughter" or "pearl of the Baltic" for a reason. Located in the far south of Finland, the city, which is made up of over 330 islands, is surrounded by sea on three sides. And while this means delicious fish, stunning views and beautiful natural landscapes, there's much more to experience in this underrated, vibrant metropolis.

In Denmark and Norway, the word is "hygge". In Sweden it's "mys". Both represent the cosy, warm feeling you get when you are happy. They don't have the same word in Finland. Instead, they have "kalsarikannit," which loosely translates as sitting drinking in your underwear. This comfortable happiness or laidback way of life is probably why Finland has been ranked as one of the happiest places to live by the UN's World Happiness Report and is another reason to visit its capital. Helsinki may not be particularly known worldwide for its sights, but it's the experiences that really make this city worth visiting.

And where better to experience that feeling of warm relaxation than a sauna? For most Finns, the sauna is like their second home and you're spoiled for choice in Helsinki. Located in Kauppatori Market Square in the heart of the city, Allas Sea Pool not only has a sauna and warm water pool, but a cold seawater pool looking over the Baltic. For a similar modern complex that's a bit more tranquil, try Löyly on the Hernesaari waterfront in the south. If you want to soak in some history as well as steam, Kotiharjun, which opened in 1928, is the oldest and last remaining public wood-fired sauna in the city. It's also located in the Bohemian district of Kallio, which is known for its relaxed atmosphere, art and food.

Which leads us onto Helsinki's cuisine. Finland is known for simple, seasonal food with a focus on fresh, locally sourced, sustainable produce. With over 100 kilometres (62 miles) of coast, fish is always on the menu. Try the Lohikeitto (salmon soup), pickled herring with new potatoes or rye bread or kalakukko (fish pie). Other traditional fare includes poronkäristys (sautéed reindeer), grillimakkara (grilled sausages), karjalanpiirakka (breakfast pastries) or puolukkapiirakka (lingonberry pie) to name a few.

It's not only food that's part of the Finnish way of life. The Finns drink more coffee per person than anywhere else on earth so, as you can imagine, the cafe culture is huge. There are even Finnish words for the coffee drunk at different times of the day including "aamukahvi"

"Finland has been ranked as one of the happiest places to live by the UN"

Helsinki cathedral is one of the architectural gems of the city

Essential information

Remember to check ahead for opening times. Some attractions are closed during winter, and museums and galleries may close on Mondays and cafes on Sundays.

Best time to visit From May to September for the best weather. During the summer for midnight sun (19 hours of daylight)

Currency € · Euro

Time zone UTC+2

NORTH

Cafe culture is a big part of life in Helsinki whether your preference is the traditional Regatta Cafe or the quirkier Moomin Cafe

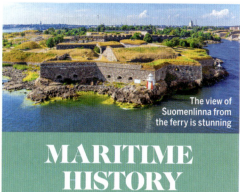

The view of Suomenlinna from the ferry is stunning

MARITIME HISTORY

Helsinki is made up of about 330 islands and while there's not time to visit them all, it's worth taking a day trip to see some of them. Suomenlinna is a sea fortress situated over eight islands joined by bridges just south of Helsinki. It started being built by the Swedish in 1748 as a defence against Russian invasion and was originally called Sveaborg. It was renamed by the Finns in 1917 and was listed as a UNESCO World Heritage site in 1991 due to the importance of its military architecture. As well as the fortress itself and breathtaking sea views, you can visit the village, museums, bunkers, cannons and the only remaining WWII submarine in Finland. The fortress is a 15-20 minute ferry ride from Market Square and there is no entrance fee so all you need to pay is the price of the ferry and anything you want from the cafe.

(morning coffee), "päiväkahvi" (day coffee), "iltakahvi" (evening coffee) and "saunakahvi" (sauna coffee). There are plenty of cafes no matter your itinerary. If you're visiting Sibelius monument, try the iconic and Instagrammable Cafe Regatta, a quaint red hut that is known for its cinnamon buns. Engel cafe, which sits opposite the Helsinki Cathedral, not only serves good coffee but it's inside one of the oldest buildings in the capital. If you fancy something a bit more quirky, why not try the Moomin Cafe? Moomin creator Tove Jansson was from Helsinki and it's said every Finn has a Moomin mug in their house so it's not just a trend, but a fun part of the culture too!

So far you've relaxed at a sauna, eaten good food and drunk good coffee, but what else makes Finland such a happy nation? Could it be the clean air? Helsinki is one of the greenest cities in Europe, with a third of it dedicated to green spaces. Everywhere you look there's a slice of nature, whether it's the sea that surrounds it, parks, nature reserves or forest. Helsinki Central Park is a 10-kilometre-long forested area that runs the length of the city and is a popular recreation ground for its walking and running trails, cycling or just spending time in the great outdoors. In the centre of the city, Esplanade Park is one of Finland's most popular green spaces, where people picnic and go to watch shows and concerts. And if you've got green fingers or want to take a stroll among a rose garden or exotic plants, check out the Winter Garden. Further afield, a day trip to Nuuksio National Park, about half an hour outside of Helsinki, is perfect for nature lovers.

While Finland may not be famous for its landmarks, this doesn't mean it's short of sights to see. The capital, known for its minimalist style, is rich in its art, design and architecture. In fact it's home to the highest concentration of Art Nouveau architecture in Europe. Some of the best examples of this include the beautiful Helsinki Central Station, famous for its two stone guards holding globes, the National Theatre, the oldest Finnish-speaking working theatre, the National Museum and Kallio Church.

But Art Nouveau is not the only style of architecture. From the functionalist Amos Rex Art Museum to the modernist Helsinki Central Library and Temppeliaukio rock church to the Neoclassical Helsinki Cathedral and the Byzantine Russian-style Uspenski Cathedral, Helsinki boasts multiple architectural styles.

Helsinki is also a UNESCO City of Design. You can explore the museums, art galleries, photography, sculptures, antiques and fashion stores of the design district to get a taste of its creative side.

While Helsinki is Finland's largest city, it's still small enough to get around by foot. You can also travel by bus, metro, rail or ferry but the best way to see the sights is on one of the oldest tram systems in the world.

Stockholm may be the home of Abba, Copenhagen the city of fairytales, but if you're looking to visit a Scandinavian city, Helsinki has just as much to offer, with fewer tourists to compete with. Just like its nickname, it's the pearl in an oyster – a hidden gem.

Useful sites
www.hsl.fi/en/tickets-and-fares/day-tickets
jt-line.fi/eng/
www.gocity.com/helsinki/en-us

Allas Sea Pool in the heart of the city has not only a sauna and pool, but a cafe, restaurant, terraces and a concert venue

COPENHAGEN

DISCOVER SCANDI STYLE IN THE CONSTANTLY EVOLVING DANISH CAPITAL

Big isn't always best and espite being one of the smallest capital cities in western Europe, Copenhagen regularly tops polls of the most desirable places to live. A day or two spent here and it soon becomes obvious why.

With its compact size, flat terrain and a profusion of cycle paths to follow, few cities are better set up for two-wheeled journeys. Join the waves of rush-hour cycle commuters on a bike tour, a quick-and-easy way to see the main sights. Among the highlights is the residence of the royal family, the Amalienborg Palace. Arrive at noon to see the changing of the guard on the octagonal courtyard between four identical palace buildings. The maintenance of tradition is less of a priority at Christiania, a self-governing free town established by hippies squatting in an abandoned army barracks in the 1970s. Graffiti-daubed, self-built homes share space with colourful converted military buildings. Locals not only sell art and crafts to the visitors who wander their streets, they also openly tout cannabis, despite the fact that it is illegal in Denmark. It's a remarkable contrast to the pomp and formality of the royal quarter.

Copenhagen is constantly rejuvenating its long-lived reputation as a centre of style. The city's cutting-edge restaurants have won 15 Michelin stars and a host of boutique shops have sprung up in Strøget, Pisserenden and the Latin Quarter. One of the best places to see the effortlessly cool locals pass by is from a cafe near the brightly painted canal-front houses of Nyhavn. Among the former residents of this pretty street is Hans Christian Andersen, who penned several of his fairy tales behind the door of number 20.

A short walk away is Tivoli Gardens, the second-oldest amusement park in the world. Contrast the Rutschebanen, a wooden rollercoaster constructed in 1914 that weaves in and out of a snow-capped mountain, with the modern metallic loops of The Demon. So impressed was an American animator who visited in the middle of the 20th century that he headed back home and began planning his own version: Disneyland. Tivoli has avoided sprawling into the kind of enormous and overwhelming tourist trap that many of its imitators have become, and the city around it is the same. Compact Copenhagen combines a small-town feeling with interesting attractions and a laid-back style. Those polls aren't wrong – to borrow the slogan of the city's brewery, it's probably the best city in the world.

Useful sites
www.visitcopenhagen.com
www.visitdenmark.com/denmark/destinations/copenhagen
www.tivoli.dk/en/

Essential information

Many museums offer free entry once a week, usually on Wednesdays.

Best time to visit May to August
Currency kr · Danish Krone
Time zone UTC+2

Ample bike parks and paths make Copenhagen a two-wheel-friendly city

The coloured gable houses along Nyhavn are perhaps Copenhagen's most iconic sight

NORTH

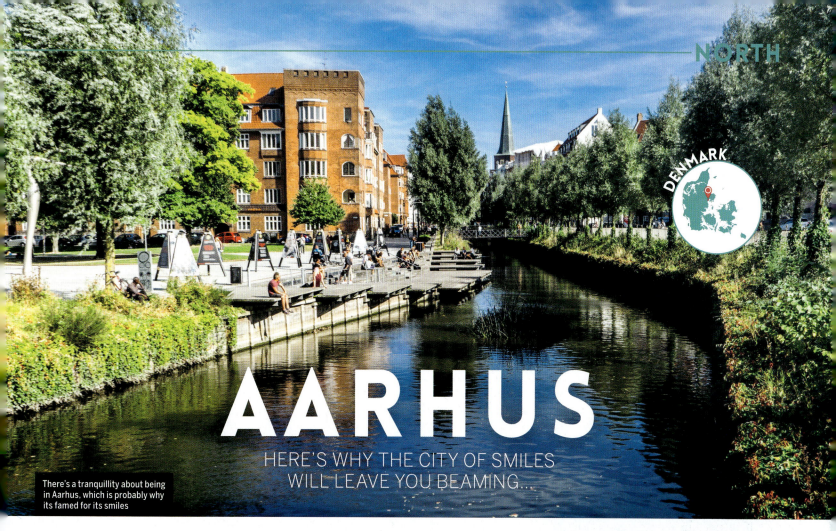

AARHUS

HERE'S WHY THE CITY OF SMILES WILL LEAVE YOU BEAMING...

There's a tranquillity about being in Aarhus, which is probably why its famed for its smiles

First off, let's set things straight: you're probably saying it wrong. Aarhus is actually how the Danes spell the city with an anglicised alphabet, but the truth is it's technically Århus– and that letter is pronounced more like 'au' as in aubergine than 'ah' as in Argyle. That makes it *or-hus* and not *are-hus*. Any Dane would forgive a foreign mishap with their language, but it's always nice to make an effort. Especially as Aarhus is the kind of place that surprises most visitors with its warm welcome, rich art and design scene, and plenty of gastronomic delights to seek out. And since it's only a three-hour train ride from Copenhagen, there's not really an excuse to miss out on the City of Smiles.

There's a uniqueness about the city that is lost in a lot of European cities, and strolling these streets will inspire thanks to its laid-back atmosphere and artistic core values. Its range is impressive, mixing modern with medieval and minimalist with artistic. There are the multicoloured properties of the harbourside and main shopping street, through to cobbled streets of the Latin quarter and the ramshackle idylls of the old town open-air museum. The iconic town hall is worth a stop for its original functionalist design, as is the equally reputed rainbow panorama walkway of the ARoS museum of art. It's a cliché to say it, but Aarhus really is one of the places where you'll want to snap a photo down practically every street. It's lush, too, with plenty of green spaces, open water and not too much interference from road traffic. In fact, Aarhus has a free bike rental scheme, meaning you can stop by any of the 56 stands in the city, grab a bike and tour these gorgeous streets.

But all that quaint Danish beauty is going to leave you peckish, and luckily that's an area that the Danes – and Aarhus in particular – are well-equipped to cater for. It's a foodie haven (to use a Danish word), and there are even food walk tours dedicated to unearthing the many aspects of Aarhus gastronomy. Street food markets have been popping up all over Denmark, creating dining hotspots with an automatic bit of flair. The one in Aarhus is no different, built into an old bus garage and housing over 30 stalls from across a broad spectrum of international tastes. Conversely, Nordic cuisine has taken hold of Aarhus as it has in a lot of the Scandinavian countries, so you'll find numerous places that offer locally sourced and seasonally available ingredients, not to mention three Michelin-star restaurants in the city. You'll eat well here, that's for sure.

The ARoS art museum is worth a visit on its own, but must go for its rainbow, rooftop panorama

Aarhus is small, all things considered, but there's more than enough that will keep you hooked – and that's even before you consider the nearby attractions, such as the royal Marselisborg Palace or the Tivoli Friheden theme park, It's called the City of Smiles for a reason, and you like to smile, don't you?

Useful sites
www.visitaarhus.com/aarhus-region
www.donkey.bike/cities/bike-rental-aarhus

Essential information

It might go against your basic instincts, but in Denmark there isn't an expectation to tip your waiters or servers.

Best time to visit Summer
Time zone UTC+1
Currency kr • Danish Krone

"It's lush, with plenty of green spaces, open water and not too much traffic"

REYKJAVÍK

JOURNEY TO ICELAND'S CAPITAL TO EXPERIENCE BREATHTAKING SCENERY AND SPECTACULAR NATURAL WONDERS

Reykjavík is a city like no other. With its magnificent backdrop of mountains and location along Iceland's south-western shoreline, embracing the constantly changing climate of the capital is all part and parcel of visiting this exciting destination.

The city is a cultural hub for those looking to get more familiar with Icelandic history, as well as its modern way of life. Featuring a wide array of museums to suit everybody's tastes, from The Settlement Exhibition, the Saga Museum and The National Gallery of Iceland, to the Whales of Iceland exhibition and the Reykjavík Museum of Photography, you're never without somewhere to visit on rainy days.

Divulge your taste buds in some of the best fish and chips at the Reykjavík Fish Restaurant along the harbour, or chomp on a fresh hot dog at the little Bæjarins Beztu Pylsur stall. If you're feeling adventurous, try out some of Iceland's more traditional delicacies, including fermented shark (hákarl), lamb soup (kjötsúpa) and dried fish (harðfiskur).

You can't visit Reykjavik without dipping your toes into a geothermal pool for instant relaxation and to soothe those sore muscles. The popular Blue Lagoon lies just a 50-minute drive away from the city centre, and will set you back around £70 ($95) entry per person. Or, for a budget-friendly alternative, locate one of the city's public swimming complexes, for example Vesturbæjarlaug, to enjoy a variety of hot pools at various temperatures for a fee of just £6 ($8) entry for adults.

Visit a Reykjavík Roasters café to slake your thirst for caffeine and enjoy expertly made coffee that will leave a lasting impression. Be wary, though, as shopping in Iceland comes with a hefty price tag. Sticking to a budget and looking for those deals where possible will make pennies stretch further. Use the AppyHour app to give you a list of all the pubs and restaurants that have deals running on drinks at any one time.

Treat the capital as a base to explore the rest of the country from, as most of Iceland's sights can be accessed through either organised tours or by hiring a rental car. A couple of days is all that's required to explore the city's highlights before heading out into the wild to witness majestic glaciers, gigantic waterfalls and exploding geysers.

Take a day out to explore the Golden Circle; a round-up of some of Iceland's most spectacular natural wonders. Sights include the stunning Thingvellir National Park that, when visited during the snowy season, is truly a winter wonderland. Also featured on the tour is Gullfoss, a huge waterfall fed from a glacier that's visible in the background on a clear day.

A northern lights tour is a must. Typically lasting three to five hours, don't forget to take your camera to capture the colourful natural wonder in all its glory – although buying photos from your tour organiser is often an option.

The fact that the number of tourists who visit Iceland each year outweighs the country's actual population by six times over is evident of just how popular this island has become as a destination to not miss out on.

Useful sites
www.grapevine.is
www.icelandtravel.is
www.local-iceland-tours.com

Mountains set the scene in this culturally rich city, with plenty for adults and children to explore

Essential information

Book a northern lights tour early in your trip, to allow for re-booking if needed.

Best time to visit May to September (for more hours of daylight)

Currency kr • Icelandic Krone

Time zone UTC

NORTH

It's primarily baroque architecture throughout Vilnius, but it has its fair share of interesting structures

VILNIUS

THE CLOSEST A CAPITAL CITY CAN GET TO BEING A HIDDEN GEM…

The Baltics are in a sort of hot trend, at the moment. The region itself has been fairly undervalued when it comes to tourism, and that has seen a major increase in the last few years. For Lithuania, that largely means its capital Vilnius has started to receive some attention from the international masses, and for good reason. It offers a lot of what an avid traveller might look for in a city escape: culture, history, a unique identity and plenty of great coffeeshops. And because it isn't quite on the same level as the likes of Rome, Paris or Berlin, Vilnius is quite considerably more affordable and less densely packed with wide-eyed tourists than any of Europe's more well-known destinations – helping it to maintain its status as a hidden gem.

The thing that most people talk of when they talk of Vilnius is, however, not technically even a part of Vilnius, at least not any more. The neighbourhood of Užupis, meaning "across the river" in Lithuanian, declared itself its own free republic in 1997 and has ever since maintained its own independence from the city. It has its own constitution, its own flag and its own president, and a rather sizable artistic community. It was artists who originally turned the abandoned and derelict neighbourhood into their homes by squatting, and now roughly 1/7th of the inhabitants here are artists of one breed or another. Much like Freetown Christiania in Copenhagen, this is a place that is unique to explore thanks to the creativity, humour and happiness of those that help to keep Užupis a thing. Check out the angel statue and the republic's rather fun constitution in the square after crossing the bridge.

That's not to say that Vilnius proper doesn't have enough to show of its own. The Old Town is a UNESCO heritage site, and its scrawling, winding cobbled streets give it exactly the kind of kitsch, romantic feel that you'd expect from a capital as comparatively small as this one. There's a notable beer culture in the city, too, with a wide variety of options on tap for tasting. Finding a trendy bar serving local ales and beer is not going to be hard while wandering these streets, though the low-key Bambalynė and Šnekutis are both good choices to aim for. The latter is particularly handy if you're also up for sampling cepelinai, since the Lithuanian national dish of potato dumplings stuffed with pork is available here.

You'll have no trouble finding your way to the main landmarks of the city, but it's also worth spending some time without a destination in mind to just wind your way beside the Vilnia River, which is actually what the city is named after and is in fact smaller than the second river that flows through the capital – the Neris River. It'll offer a different, more chilled vibe than most city breaks offer, and honestly, that's something that can be said for Vilnius as a whole.

Useful sites
www.govilnius.lt/visit-vilnius
www.uzupiorespublika.com/en/home/
www.vilnius-events.lt/en/

Essential information

1 April is Užupis Independence Day, and it's the only day you can get an Užupis stamp in your passport.

Best time to visit Aside from 1 April for Užupis Day, travel between June and August for warmer days

Time zone UTC+1

Currency € · Euro

There are plenty of churches, museums and galleries to explore, but a surprisingly rich pub culture too

The rooftops of Tallinn, with the Gulf of Finland of the Baltic Sea in the background

TALLINN

IMMERSION IN THE MIDDLE AGES HAS NEVER FELT SO REAL

With cobblestone streets, medieval churches and beautifully preserved 13th-century origins, Tallinn is a history lover's – and tourist trap avoider's – panacea. Visit the Raeapteek for the oldest continuously operating pharmacy in Europe, already on its third owner by 1422, or the cobblestone cross in Town Hall Square where mythology and fact collide. The 70-hectare Kadriorg Park is ideal for a moment of peace, whether you're drawn to the palatial views, flower gardens, forest groves, Japanese garden, or Swan Pond with its gazebo, fountain and birds. In spring, don't miss the park's blossoming cherry trees.

Particularly interesting is Kiek in de Kök, translated from Low German as 'peep into the kitchen' – an intriguing tower which allowed occupants to see into the kitchens of nearby houses, now serving as a photography museum and offering panoramic views of the Old Town from the top-floor cafe. The whole-museum ticket for £10 ($12) includes admission to the Maiden, Stable and Gate towers, as well as the bastion passages and Carved Stone Museum.

If you feel like exploring, the Estonian Open Air Museum on the outskirts of Tallinn provides a different view of the country's history, at £10 ($12) in summer and £9 ($10) in winter, with the possibility of a combo ticket with Tallinn Zoo. Back in the city, the 2.5-kilometre (1.5-mile) Cultural Kilometre offers visitors the city via the road less travelled. Expect strange Soviet structures, old factories-cum-museums, unsettling bunkers covered in graffiti, a fish market and a wealth of street art. The Patarei Prison and Sea Fortress stands out along the way, with access to cells, exercise yards, the medical wing and hanging rooms which don't look dissimilar to *American Horror Story*. Even if the series isn't familiar, you can imagine the disturbing visuals.

Essential information

Purchase the Tallinn Card, starting from £23 ($27), for free public transport and generous discounts.

Best time to visit May-June (to avoid the peak tourist season)

Currency € · Euro

Time zone UTC+2

On a lighter note, for period music, traditional dress and a taste of Tallinn's medieval fare, visit the 17th-century Pakkhoone at Vene 1 in the Old Town for the Olde Hansa restaurant. The whole menu uses 15th-century recipes for dishes, such as oven-baked herb and juniper cheese, Osilia freshwater trout, Reval's meat tasting plate, Earl's forest mushroom soup and rose pudding dessert, topped off with warm herb schnapps, light cinnamon beer or a selection of spiced wines. While Olde Hansa could be considered a tourist trap, it's authentic and deserves to be as popular as it is. For an alternative, more authentic local feel, visit the Bohemian Kalamaja just outside of the Old Town, a former fisherman's district of old wooden houses and traditional industries juxtaposed with locally frequented pubs, restaurants, coffee shops and flea markets.

Lastly, if you want to go further afield, ferry trips to Helsinki from £33 ($39) for a return and take around two hours – for a cultural day trip, why not? Head to page 30 to find out why the Finnish capital is worth a trip!

Useful sites
www.visittallinn.ee/eng
www.oldehansa.ee
www.linnamuuseum.ee/en/

Christmastime in Tallinn Old Town. In 2022, Tallinn was named one of Europe's top seven Christmas markets

NORTH

LATVIA

RIGA

THIS CITY HAS BECOME POPULAR AS A HIP AND STYLISH CENTRE, WITH A YOUTH AND VIBRANCY THAT SITS WELL WITH ITS HERITAGE

Riga is a double capital – watching not only over Latvia but also the Baltics as a whole, so encompassing Estonia and Lithuania as well. It's a good idea to start in the old town with a visit to St Peter's Church and an ascent of its tower to admire views of the city and the Daugava River snaking through.

St Peter's is one of the oldest buildings in Riga, although the bits visible today are comparatively modern and hail from the 15th and 17th centuries. While St Peter's might be the more famous church, the main Riga Cathedral is actually a nearby beautiful 13th-century landmark; look out for its massive organ and medieval cloisters.

Stroll around the main square in the old town and it won't take long for you to imagine life in medieval times – they've always been a meeting place but we can't help but think the café offerings have vastly improved over the centuries. The show-stealer is the House of Blackheads, a double-fronted building with stepped gables that zing against a blue Latvian sky. In total contrast is the big black block of the Museum of the Occupation of Latvia; it's a visual and emotive reminder of Latvia's 20th-century history and its 50-year occupation.

Other highlights of the old town include checking out what remains of the town walls and Swedish Gate, walking down the narrow Rozena Street, and admiring the arts and crafts houses on Skarnu Street. Finally, don't miss the Three Brothers in Maza Pils Street, three wonderfully wonky houses that each come from a different period of history and now house the Latvian Museum of Architecture.

It's not all ancient history, and there is plenty more to see in Riga from the last century or so. Take, for instance, the Freedom Monument, a symbol of the Latvian people's desire for independence and love. There's also the National Library of Latvia on the banks of the river, also known as the Castle of Light thanks to its luminescent peaked design, which contrasts fully with the charming wooden dwellings you find nearby.

Our final word on architecture goes to Art Nouveau. There are reported to be over 300 Art Nouveau buildings in Latvia, about a third of which are in the city centre. For a good concentration of them, head to Alberta Street and indulge your passion further by visiting the Art Nouveau Museum.

When it comes to art, the Latvian Museum of Art is a top pick. It's housed in an elegant and formal building with modern extensions and roof terraces, but if you like something more independent, you'll be pleased to hear that Riga is also making a name for itself in modern art, by filling Soviet-era industrial buildings with small pop-ups.

Riga has much to offer in terms of Scandi-style and cosy cafes. There are also some interesting culinary trends, and the Riga Central Market is a good place to start your foray into sour pickles and smoked eels. Like many cities in Europe, artisanal beer is in the midst of an upswing, and microbreweries and brewpubs have taken over the site of a 19th-century brewery in Beer District.

Useful sites
www.latvia.travel/en/city/riga
www.latvia.travel/en
www.opera.lv/en/home

Essential information

Riga has an excellent network of trams and buses operating from 5am to midnight.

Best time to visit Summer temperatures are low to mid 20s

Currency € · Euro

Time zone UTC+2

The step-gabled beauty that is the House of Blackheads

Riga's cobblestoned old town is a UNESCO World Heritage Site

Sveiki!

SOUTH

40 Rome
42 Milan
43 Parma
44 Florence
45 Bologna
46 Cremona
48 Naples
49 Matera
50 Venice
52 Palermo
53 Seville
54 Barcelona
56 Valencia
57 Palma De Mallorca
58 San Sebastián
59 Madrid
60 Bilbao
61 Porto
62 Lisbon
64 Athens
65 Kavala
66 Thessaloniki
67 Valletta

ROME

VISIT THE STUNNING CAPITAL OF ITALY AND EXPERIENCE A PART OF HISTORY

Italy's capital will take you on a journey into the past while enabling you to enjoy the cosmopolitan buzz of a fashionable city. Explore ancient Roman ruins, soak up the art and culture, and enjoy the incredible cuisine.

Begin your day with a trip to the Colosseum, then take a walk through the Roman Forum and on to the Pantheon. The Colosseum is a spectacle not to be missed – it's the largest amphitheatre ever built, and still an icon of Imperial Rome. Even if you don't want to venture inside, you'll really regret not taking the time to see it in person. The area around it can feel a little daunting; the roads are wide and busy, but there are some lovely restaurants close by where you can enjoy a traditional lasagne with a view of the spectacular structure. The Colosseum is striking at any time of day, but imagine sitting in view of it with a glass of Italian wine as the sun sets and streams through its many arches. We really can't think of many things better than starting and ending your day at this stunning building.

The Roman Forum is another iconic landmark of the Roman Empire. It's filled with temples, squares and old government buildings that are well worth taking a stroll around. You can explore it alone or join a tour to learn about the interesting history of the site. Nearby the Pantheon is a 2,000-year-old temple, the best preserved of all of Rome's ancient monuments. It is one of the most influential buildings in the Western world. Venturing through its large, bronze doors and into the largest unreinforced concrete dome ever built is probably as awe-inspiring and breathtaking as it was when it was first constructed. Despite its age, it's still as stunning as ever.

Vatican City, the independent city-state, is the headquarters of the Roman Catholic Church. A trip to the Vatican should be left for a day when you have nothing else planned, as there is a lot to see. It's home to St Peter's Basilica and the Vatican Museums, which contain artistic masterpieces such as Michelangelo's Sistine Chapel frescoes.

The Vatican is by far the city's most popular tourist destination, so be prepared for a lot of people and many, many queues. If this fills you with dread, just be sure to avoid Wednesdays, as this is usually when the Papal Audience takes place. This is when the Pope is in Rome, meaning there will be even more people. In the warmer months, this is often held in St Peter's Square, so if you do want to get a glimpse of the Pope then head on down – just prepare yourself for a lot of people around! Visiting the Vatican Museums with a tour is by far the best way to do it, and between April and October you can book to visit the museum at night, which means there are fewer people to cope with. If you plan on visiting St Peter's Basilica, then you must be dressed appropriately – no bare knees, midriffs or shoulders on show.

The most popular square in Rome, Piazza Navona, shouldn't be left off your itinerary. The piazza is lined with restaurants, cafes and

Make a wish at this fountain and all of your dreams might come true

You can't move in Rome without a picture-perfect vista in your sights

SOUTH

Take a wander around the old government buildings of ancient Rome

The Colosseum: one of the most iconic sights of Rome

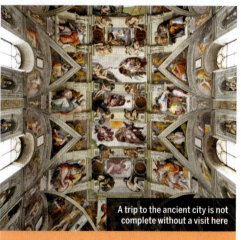

A trip to the ancient city is not complete without a visit here

THE SISTINE CHAPEL

Visit the official residence of the Pope situated in the Apostolic Palace. The stunning chapel was originally called Cappella Magna and was named after Pope Sixtus IV, who restored it between 1477 and 1480. You can book tickets in advance in order to skip the queues and secure entry into an often-sold-out venue. It's located within the Vatican Museums, and access to the Sistine Chapel is included with your museum tickets. The Sistine Chapel is the last room you'll visit on your trip through the museums and the 54 galleries. They truly leave the best until last on this tour. It's absolutely stunning and very memorable.

> *"There are many pretty fountains to be found in the city's piazzas"*

swanky shops to explore – but it will definitely burn a hole in your wallet! The ornate fountain, Fontana dei Quattro Fiumi, sits at its centre too. Another piazza not to forget about is Piazza di Spagna, which is where the city's famous Spanish Steps are. It's a central meeting place for both locals and tourists, and a great place for people-watching and candid photography.

In the evening, take a romantic walk to the famous Trevi Fountain, and make a wish by throwing a coin in using your right hand over your left shoulder – a tradition at the fountain. Standing 26 metres (85 feet) tall and 49 metres (161 feet) wide, it is the largest Baroque fountain in the city. There are many pretty fountains to be found in the city's piazzas where you can enjoy a delicious Italian coffee, sample crisp white wine from the nearby Castelli Romani hills, and make sure you don't miss out on trying the gelato. On the way to the Trevi Fountain you'll stumble across Giolitti, which is Rome's oldest and best gelateria – well worth the pit stop.

After a long day exploring the once 'caput mundi' (capital of the world), enjoy watching the world go by in one of the pizzerias or trattorias located within the many piazzas. Don't forget to sample traditional dishes that can only be truly enjoyed in Rome. Seek out a proper Roman carbonara, made with just a handful of ingredients, or look for the classic amatriciana, made with a rich tomato sauce and savoury pork cheek. Start your day with a local maritozzo, which is a sweet, yeasty bun containing raisins and pine nuts and filled with delicious whipped cream.

Useful sites
www.vaticantickets.org
www.rome.info
www.colosseum-rome-tickets.com

Essential information

Watch out for pickpockets, especially around busy piazzas and packed tourist destinations.

Best time to visit April to October (if you want to see the Pope!)

Currency € · Euro

Time zone UTC+1

The canals in the Navigli district of Milan are a popular spot for drinks, food and nightlife

MILAN

THIS NORTH ITALIAN CITY IS PEERLESS WHEN IT COMES TO ART AND DESIGN – IT'S NOT BAD FOR A SPOT OF RETAIL THERAPY EITHER

While Milan hasn't got the headliner appeal of Rome or Florence, it's absolutely stuffed with things to do. Because it's a large city, it's wise to plan ahead… so let's start with the big hitters you need to book online beforehand.

There are three sights we recommend booking in advance. First up, the spiky Duomo di Milano, a must-visit 14th-century cathedral that took 600 years to make, and boasts more statues than any other cathedral in the world. You may be able to snaffle some tickets on the day but if you buy ahead you'll skip the long queues. Now for the biggy: Leonardo's *The Last Supper*. Buy your tickets for this uber-famous masterpiece a few weeks in advance – and maybe more if you're going in summer. Third on the list of book-ahead experiences is the world-famous Milanese opera house, La Scala – but only if you're visiting during opera season, which runs between December and June.

Of course, Milan is about way more than big-budget sights; in fact, many of its loveliest corners are al fresco, including the Monumental Cemetery. This is not only the final resting place of many famous Italians but also a visual feast with its fantastically decorated tombs. Then there is Sforza Castle, an impressive 15th-century fortification located just outside the historical centre.

One of our favourite areas is Navigli, where two of the city's canals converge. It's a quiet area during the day but comes alive when the after-work aperitivo culture gets going, and bar owners serve seemingly endless drinks and complementary small plates. You can also take bikes from here on the Naviglio Martesana, a 100 percent canal-path route from Milan to Cassano d'Adda.

Milan is an amazing place for art lovers, and its works span many centuries, from *The Last Supper* right up to Maurizio Cattelan's middle-finger sculpture of 2010. The arresting fist sits in Milan's financial district and seems to be a comment on bankers' responsibility for recent financial crises. Hangar Bicocca is a popular contemporary artspace, an erstwhile locomotive manufacturing plant in the north of the city, and there's Fondazione Prada, another gallery this time housed in an old distillery and showing a mix of temporary exhibitions and permanent works from artists like Louise Bourgeois and Dan Flavin. Fans of Wes Anderson will be delighted by the bar he designed on the premises – Bar Luce. Pinacoteca di Brera is a great gallery that shows Italian paintings all the way through from the 14th to the 20th century.

Design lovers will also find a lot to like. The Triennale di Arte Decorativa showcases the history of Italian design, while The Armani/Silos shows hundreds of the designer's sartorial hits. And don't forget that Milan is a great place to shop, from the designer stores in the glass-vaulted Galleria Vittorio Emanuele II, which links Piazza del Duomo and the Piazza della Scala, to Corso di Porta Ticinese and its Portobello Road vibe.

Useful sites
yesmilano.it/en
cenacolovinciano.org/en/
teatroallascala.org/

Essential information

The MilanoCard includes transport, audioguide and discounted entry to many attractions.

Best time to visit Spring and Autumn
Currency € · Euro
Time zone UTC+1

SOUTH

PARMA

PARMA IS SMALL BUT MIGHTY – ESPECIALLY WHEN IT COMES TO CURED MEAT AND CRUMBLY CHEESE

How long can you live on ham and cheese alone? We're not sure but a city break's worth of time is definitely possible when you're talking about the nutty, saltiness of Parmesan cheese and the rich unctuous moreishness of Parma ham.

Parma is part of the Emilia-Romagna region in northern Italy, an area known for its hefty contribution to Italy's gastronomic might, with around a third of its labour force working in the agri-food and food industries. In fact, it has a UNESCO inscription as a Creative City of Gastronomy, and counts high-quality Culatello di Zibello (cured meat), the Porcini Mushroom di Borgotaro, Coppa di Parma (sausage), Tortelli d'erbetta (pasta) alongside the aforementioned Parma ham and Parmigiano Reggiano, as well as numerous wines from neighbouring hills, as part of its arsenal.

A city break in Parma is likely then to be dominated by food and you'll be spoilt for choice when it comes to cookery classes, foodie tours and visits to producers. A good example is Parmesan; taking a dairy tour in a local Agricola (farm) will have you pulling on a hairnet and wellies, learning about the cheese-making process and finding out how the specific bacteria in Parmese soil creates the perfect taste. You may even be allowed to shave off a bit of fresh cheese on your way through the storeroom.

If just eating food is enough for you, Parma serves up a vast array of restaurants and bars and a good starting point for visitors is Piazza Garibaldi, especially if you touch down late afternoon. Every evening at 6pm – or aper-o'clock – the square comes alive with people in search of an evening drink and snack.

So, once the appetite is sated, and you want to walk off your excesses, what else does Parma have to offer? Unsurprisingly, it's very old and very beautiful: its amber buildings glow in the sun and its amazing domes create beautiful silhouettes in the sunset skies.

Start with a trio of treats in the form of the Baptistery, the city cathedral and the San Giovanni Evangelista church. All three nestle close together in the Piazza Duomo, the Baptistery's medieval pink marble marvel towering high above, the centuries-old cathedral boasting renaissance frescoes and the newer (16th century) San Giovanni Evangelisa quietly offering up its beautiful cloister for a bit of peace and quiet. Beyond these beauties, you should also check out the Teatro Farnese, an ancient and overblown vanity project of elaborate decoration that was destroyed in WWII but has been rebuilt since in exacting detail. Expect columns, porticos and more besides.

Parco Ducale, just beyond Ponte Giuseppe Verdi, is a lovely way to spend a lazy afternoon, whether it's a post-prandial snooze you're after, or a bit of innocent people-watching.

Useful sites
parmacityofgastronomy.it/en/
emiliaromagnaturismo.it/en/towns/parma
emiliaromagnaturismo.it/en

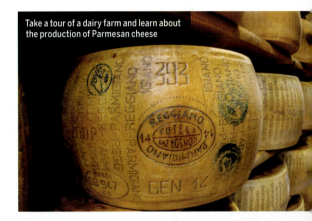

Take a tour of a dairy farm and learn about the production of Parmesan cheese

Essential information

Italian custom is to serve crisps, olives and sometimes meat and cheese with an early drink, or aperitivo.

Best time to visit Late spring
Currency € · Euro
Time zone UTC+1

Parma's Piazza Duomo and its cathedral and Baptistery

FLORENCE

A SHRINE TO THE RENAISSANCE ERA, THIS CITY IS BRIMMING WITH ART AND CULTURE

This historic Italian city, nestled in the Tuscany region, is as beautiful as it is fascinating. For starters, Florence is one of the few cities on the globe whose historical centre is listed as a UNESCO World Heritage Site due to its invaluable contributions to art, history and culture. Here, art lovers and history geeks alike will find plenty to entertain them.

At the centre of the city is the Piazza della Signoria. The most famous square in Florence, it is considered the political heart of the locality, whose government operates from the neighbouring town hall, the Palazzo Vecchio. The square itself has played a vital role in many important historical moments such as the Bonfire of the Vanities in 1497, when supporters of Dominican friar Girolamo Savonarola collected and tossed thousands of objects such as cosmetics, art and books that were purported to tempt sin into a large fire pit constructed in the square.

Much like the history of Florence, the art it displays is famous across the globe. Inside the Uffizi Gallery, which is just minutes from the square, is a rare gem of 15th-century Renaissance art and one of Botticelli's finest pieces: The Birth of Venus. Approximately two kilometres (1.2 miles) away, inside the Galleria dell'Accademia, visitors can gaze upon Michelangelo's famous David statue, which he carved from a single block of marble in the early 16th century at the age of just 26.

Approximately 450 metres from the gallery, situated at the centre of the city's main market district, you will find the church of San Lorenzo, one of Florence's biggest churches and said to have been consecrated by St Ambrose on Easter Day, 393 CE. This impressive monument also contains the Medici Chapel, the famous mausoleum of the Medici family — the most powerful and influential family in Florence between the 15th and 18th centuries.

One of the greatest masterpieces of Gothic architecture to be found in Florence is the Cattedrale di Santa Maria del Fiore (the Cathedral of Saint Mary of the Flower.) This Florentine cathedral is one of the largest churches in Christianity and was a symbol of wealth and power in the city during the 13th and 14th centuries as it was the largest cathedral in Europe, with a capacity for 30,000 people. The 463 steps up the cathedral offer the best view of the city. From the top, you'll be able to take in the wondrous sight of the city, while the adjacent Giotto's Campanile (bell tower) allows for a view of Florence's famous Duomo, which is largely responsible for the iconic silhouette of the Florence skyline.

Useful sites
www.visitflorence.com
www.florence-tourism.com
www.italyheaven.co.uk/tuscany/florence/index.html

Essential information

From the main city centre, cross the river for a more authentic taste of Florence.

Best time to visit April to June
Currency € Euro
Time zone UTC+1

Surrounded by the idyllic Tuscan hills and bisected by the beautiful Arno River, Florence's Renaissance landscape has remained unchanged for centuries

SOUTH

BOLOGNA

FOOD, GLORIOUS FOOD! IN A COUNTRY THAT IS FAMED FOR ITS GASTRONOMY, BOLOGNA IS THE CHERRY ON THE CAKE

Bologna is less touristy than other Italian cities and that is one of its strengths as a weekend destination. For a start, you don't have the pressure of world-famous sights to distract you from relaxing and drinking in the beauty of Italy and secondly, it has the food. All the wonderful food!

Bologna was awash with towers in times gone by, partly as military defence but also because they were seen as boasting rights in certain social circles. Two towers remain as symbols of the city – the Torre Degli Asinelli and the Torre Garisenda – but twins they are not. Asinelli is just over twice the height of Garisenda, although the latter claims the greater lean. If you're feeling energetic, it's a great idea to scale the 498 steps of Asinelli and gaze out on the roofs of the city, letting the food smells waft up into your nostrils.

We'll get to food in a moment, but let's cover the history and architecture first. Piazza Maggiore is, as the name suggests, the main square and it's got that higgledy-piggledy charm; a beautiful mish-mash of red-brick Tuscan arches, porticos and marble-fronted buildings, all of different dimensions and eras.

It's packed with important buildings including the Palazzo d'Accursio, the Palazzo del Podesta, the Basilica di San Petronio and the Palazzo Comunale. The gothic Basilica, which dates from the late 14th century, has an unfinished part-marble façade and neighbouring Piazza del Nettuno hosts the Fountain of Neptune. You'll want to visit Archiginnasio, once a part of the University of Bologna and home to the Anatomical Theatre. The ancient wooden room has seating circling an ornate anatomical table, which is where medical students would have watched live surgery and dissections as part of their course.

Bologna is also famous for its portico – partially enclosed walkways lined with arches and columns. In fact, it boasts 40 kilometres (25 miles) of UNESCO-listed beauties including the longest in the world, which leads to the top of Monte della Guardia. It's a great walk and the tree-studded hill provides a nice spot for a shady picnic and views of the city.

Talking of picnics... it's time to talk tuck. Your trip to Bologna should centre around food; it's no accident that the city is nicknamed La Grassa – or The Fat One. Not only do you have markets like Mercato delle Erbe, Mercato di Mezzo and the old market in Quadrilatero to wander and discover, you also have shops like Atti & Figli bakery and Tamburini to peruse. Tamburini makes the local speciality, tortellini, a ring-shaped pasta filled with all sorts from cheese to veg to meat and served in a broth. For us, strolling the ancient streets and meeting the Italian producers, chefs and servers is what it's about but if you prefer a more modern approach, you could take a bus from the centre and visit FICO Eataly World. Some call it a food theme park but it's more of a centre designed to educate and inform visitors about Italian gastronomy – all under one roof.

Useful sites
www.bolognawelcome.com
emiliaromagnaturismo.it/en
www.fico.it/it

Essential information

Choose from a selection of Bologna Welcome Cards for entry to various museums and galleries and the Asinelli tower.

Best time to visit Spring and Autumn
Currency € · Euro
Time zone UTC+1

Bologna's skyline punctuated by the two towers Asinelli and Garisenda

Piazza del Comune, Cremona (you can see the duomo and its baptistry)

CREMONA

THE IDEAL CITY FOR VIOLIN AND MUSIC LOVERS TO RELAX

Founded by the Romans in 218 BC, but better known for its medieval architecture, Cremona is a rare thing – a quintessential Italian town without the crowds. With a population of 70,000, Cremona genuinely offers peace and quiet. Many travellers visiting Lombardy won't include it in their itinerary, and prefer to stop in nearby Milan or Brescia. But music lovers will know Cremona thanks to its violin-making tradition and its many luthiers' shops. It was, in fact, the home of those who detained the finest secrets of the luthier's trade since the 15th and 16th centuries: the Amati, Stradivari and Guarneri del Gesù families.

Even now, aspiring luthiers from all over the world come to Cremona to study at its violin-making schools and become internationally renowned artisans. Cremona is therefore a must-visit for classical music connoisseurs. It's home to the Violin Museum, where the history and tradition of the instrument meets the modern architecture of its auditorium. Every Saturday, one of the antique violins of the museum's collection is played for an audience, to keep the instruments in use and in tune. Theatre lovers will also appreciate the spectacular 19th-century Teatro Ponchielli, where they can see opera, ballet, concertos and plays.

The town is rather small and easy to walk around. You can go anywhere on foot, strolling through the atmospheric streets of the old district. Walk down Via Palestro to find some of Cremona's most beautiful buildings. Some of them are now schools, and you are able to walk inside and visit them. Don't miss Palazzo Stanga and its astonishing cloister. Art lovers also can't miss the picture gallery in the Ala Ponzone Museum nearby, where they'll see the iconic painting by Arcimboldo – The Gardener. When viewed upside down, it looks like a rather rude human face. Be sure to crane your neck to see it for yourself.

When visiting any ancient town in Italy, you will notice art, nature, culture, food and drink live in harmony. By peeking into the local shops you'll see Cremona's artisan traditions also include the making of cured meats, cheeses, Cremona's 'mostarda' (a pickled fruit preserve) and the local nougat, torrone. Cremona has been making torrone since 1441, when it was served at the wedding of Duke Francesco Sforza and Bianca Maria Visconti. Try it at Pasticceria Lanfranchi in Via Solferino – it's said to be the best in town. If you're

Essential information

Make sure you go down by the Po river at sunset. The view from under the bridge is absolutely breathtaking.

Best time to visit March to May for good weather

Currency € Euro

Time zone UTC+1

How to get there If travelling by plane, fly into Milan then reach Cremona by train. The train station is centrally located. If driving, Cremona is less than an hour away from Milan

Ciao!

SOUTH

The gorgeous interior of Cremona Town Hall

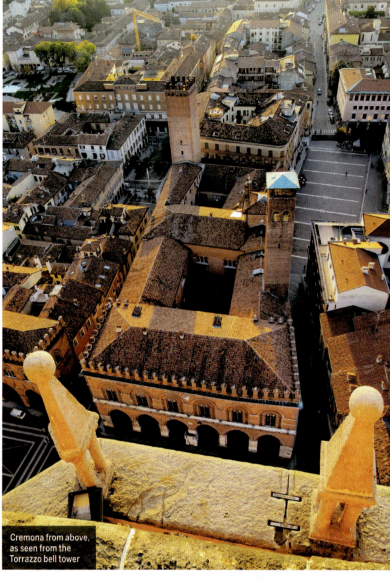

Cremona from above, as seen from the Torrazzo bell tower

"Cremona is a must-visit for classical music connoisseurs"

looking for an authentic cup of Italian coffee, have it at Tubino, one of Cremona's most historical cafés.

Cremona's beating heart is the medieval Piazza del Comune, better known as Piazza del Duomo. Here, both the medieval political and religious powers are represented, the former by the town hall and the latter by the cathedral. In the town hall, Palazzo Comunale, culture vultures will be able to visit beautifully decorated rooms, and then go on to Palazzo dei Militi next door, which is one of the town's oldest buildings.

The duomo, in the Romanesque style, was begun in the 12th century and eventually finished in the 15th century. Such is its genius that it has been dubbed by critics 'the Sistine Chapel of the Po Valley' for the intricacy of its frescoes. The octagonal baptistry, in a mixed Romanesque and Gothic style, is external. At 34 metres (112 feet) tall, its façade is covered in white marble and, together with the duomo, it provides a great contrast with Cremona's warm red brick buildings. The bell tower, known as 'Torrazzo', standing at 112 metres (367 feet) tall, is the tallest brick bell tower in Europe. By huffing and puffing up its 500 steps, one can see the whole town, with its red rooftops and the verdant countryside just beyond them. The Torrazzo is also said to have provided the inspiration for the shape and the name of the town's beloved torrone. Another great example of religious architecture is 15th-century San Sigismondo. It's located just outside the town centre, a short walk away. Its best feature is the adjacent monastery with its pleasant cloister.

Nature lovers will find an ideal setting for restorative bike rides. Cremona's luscious countryside is surrounded by four rivers: Po, Adda, Oglio and Serio. Ride your bicycle along the river banks and in the area's natural parks. After a long bike ride, relax in the evening with a drink at Molo 57 and join the night life in Piazza della Pace. Visiting in spring will enable you to find great weather: just the right time for a break in this stunning little town.

Useful sites
turismocremona.it/en
in-lombardia.it/en
enchantingitaly.com/regions/lombardia

Don't be put off by the nondescript exterior!

PIAZZA LODI

If traditional Cremonese architecture takes your fancy, you'll want to stop in sleepy Piazza Lodi to see the 17th century red brick 'Palazzo Lodi Zaccaria'. The exterior might not look instantly impressive, but don't be fooled – inside, you'll find a palace full of Doric columns and beautiful Baroque frescoes.

When in the area around lunch or dinnertime, you could stop and eat at the charming Trattoria Cerri, where the gnocchi is very popular with locals. Another popular spot is Antica Osteria del Fico, which frequently hosts lively music and dance nights. Both serve very traditional Lombardian fare.

© Images: Getty

Ciao!

NAPLES

NAPLES IS EXCITING, EXOTIC AND MAKES THE HAIRS ON THE BACK OF YOUR NECK STAND ON END

Naples has a reputation for being busy, dirty and even a bit dangerous but in reality it's an intoxicating place to visit, with its melting pot of cultures, its loud and demonstrative people and its staggering history. There's so much to see and do that it's hard to cover it all in a weekend, but here are our essential highlights.

If you fly into the airport and screech into town in one of the breakneck-speed cabs, you might not know where's north, south, east or west. A good place to orient yourself is at the docks, where you can see across the Bay of Naples to Vesuvius, Sorrento and more, as well as Naples' Castel dell'Ovo, so named because, according to legend, Roman poet Virgil put an egg in its foundations. It's the oldest fortification in Naples and has also been an island palace and prison over the centuries.

You need plenty of time to meander in the UNESCO-listed Centro Storico, the old part of the city. By day, explore the myriad ancient churches like the 15th-century Chiesa del Gesù Nuovo which, despite its austere façade, is decorated and beautiful inside. There's also Cappella Sansevero, renowned for its marble sculpture of the Veiled Christ, and the Santa Chiara religious complex, of which the colourful cloister is a highlight.

In the early evening, the historical centre is atmospheric and far less intimidating than you may have been lead to believe. Make sure you wander the Spaccanapoli, one of the many narrow streets where the opposing balconies are so close you could step from one to the other, and go to Via San Gregorio, where artisan craftspeople make presipio (nativity scenes) and Christmas figurines in workshops.

Piazza Bellini is excellent for an apero; it's lined with arsty bars and stuffed with academics and bohemians after chit-chat, romance and shade from the day's heat. Many Neapolitan soirées feature a passeggiata, an after-dinner walk that includes socialising, ice cream and the chance to parade a new family member/tech gadget/outfit. The Lungomare alongside the sea is a hotspot for locals and provides great people-watching opportunities.

Naples' main museum, the National Archaeological Museum, rivals many capital cities for its historical importance, mainly because it's where they took all the best small-scale finds from Pompeii and Herculaneum. Don't miss the Farnese Marbles, Roman copies of classical Greek sculptures, as well as ancient Roman bronzes from the Villa of the Papyri.

And now to the food. In Naples, you're in the birthplace of pizza and as such it's become something of an art form to create the lightest base and airiest sides. Everywhere you look has a pizza restaurant and you'll be very unlucky if you come across a bad one, although you might be tempted into more leftfield menu choices like pizza fritta, a deep-fried variety.

Useful sites
naplespass.eu/
www.italia.it/en/campania/naples
mann-napoli.it

Essential information

You can easily navigate Naples on foot, which is the best way to get a feel for the city.

Best time to visit Spring and autumn unless you like it hot, hot, hot!

Currency € · Euro

Time zone UTC+1

The Naples seafront and, in the distance, Vesuvius

SOUTH

MATERA

SOUTHERN ITALY'S CITY OF CAVES FROM A FANTASY WORLD

When thinking of Italy, cave dwellings carved like honeycomb into a mountain aren't likely at the front of your mind. This is where Matera gets missed, or rather, where travellers miss out on Matera. On foot, you can explore the uninhabited caves of Sasso Caveoso and the warren of Sasso Barisano, or view them from above in the violet dusk from the Crialoss Cafe; whatever your vantage point, the UNESCO World Heritage Site is unlike anything you can imagine.

Unmissable are the chiese rupestri, or rock churches. For £7 ($8), the three-church ticket includes the Santa Lucia alle Malve, notable for its art, the San Pietro Barisano, the largest and home to an unsettling crypt, and the Santa Maria de Idris, by far the most distinctive of all and reminiscent of a painting by Dali. One hundred and fifty more churches await in the Park of the Rock Churches across the river, either through a guided tour or by bike. (Note that although the tour does offer the beauty of the churches at sunset, the tour is pricey at £87 ($103) for a couple and £26 ($31) as part of a group. Conversely, bike hire from ListNRide in Matera starts from £16 ($19) a day.)

If more calls to you than the churches, the all-inclusive ticket for £17 ($20) gives you access to the above and more. The Casa Grotta, traditionally furnished one-room cave dwellings, are certainly worth visiting. While not the most popular, Casa Grotta C'era Una Volta is quiet and intriguing and usually free of crowds. The MATA museum, the Pozzo neighbourhood, and the Gathering of the Waters are also included.

Even more captivating is the Palombaro Lungo, an underground cistern frequently compared to a subterranean cathedral. Although this isn't a particularly lengthy attraction, it's absolutely worth a visit – you could have been transported to Middle Earth, such are the echoing walkways and sense of being far from civilisation.

Of course, don't forget you're in Italy, so no trip would be complete without food. Try the handmade local orecchiette and cavatelli, the "reaper's breakfast" of cialledda – bread, tomato, cucumber, pepper, and olive oil – or the strazzata, a local focaccia. Vegetarians should enjoy the crapiata, a traditional soup of grains and beans, and meat eaters the cured meats and wild boar sausage. Lastly, don't miss the Matera bread, marked until the 1950s with a wooden stamp in order to distinguish the bakers' families.

Matera itself is fully accessible without a car, and with the ZTL restrictions and permit requirement to park in the historic centre, public transport is far more convenient. The nearest airport is in Bari, 65 kilometres (40 miles) away, and from there the bus takes 75 minutes. The price depends on the time but won't leave even the most budget-conscious out of pocket.

As one of the oldest inhabited settlements in the world, you won't regret a visit to Matera.

Useful sites
www.listnride.com/matera
www.oltrelartematera.it/en/home-2/
www.infosassidimatera.com/

Essential information

🇮🇹 Stay in one of Matera's cave hotels to add to your trip's wonder.

Best time to visit
April to October

Currency € · Euro

Time zone UTC+1

Matera gorge, with a number of ancient cave dwellings carved out of the rock

Not many houses in the world have a watery back garden that is also a major highway

Ciao!

Essential information

As there are no cars in Venice, park just outside the city and get the bus into the town.

Best time to visit June to July

Currency € Euro

Time zone UTC+1

SOUTH

VENICE

NAVIGATE THE UNIQUE WATERWAYS OF ITALY'S CITY OF BRIDGES

Venice is known throughout the world as the City of Canals, among many other names. One such name is the Floating City, made up as it is of 118 islands connected by canals, which can be crossed by one of 400 bridges. It measures just eight square kilometres (three square miles), but packs an astonishing number of stunning landmarks, cafes and activities into that small space.

Conveniently, three of those landmarks are all within a couple of minutes' walk from each other – namely Doge's Palace, St Mark's Basilica and St Mark's Square.

Doge's Palace is the spectacular result of a project lasting several centuries. Started in the 9th century, the seat of the Venetian government continued to be developed and redeveloped until well into the 17th century. This drawn-out building process means that the palace features an array of architectural styles, from Gothic to Renaissance – guaranteed to delight both the casual and committed architecture enthusiast. The palace wasn't only the Venetian Parliament; it was home to the Doge, and has also acted as a prison and the city's court, but is now a fascinating museum. It may be worth more than one visit too, because the palace changes colour throughout the day depending on the light – sometimes appearing white, but other times taking on a pinkish hue. The palace is well worth a walk around, but be sure to take a look at it from the Bridge of Sighs, which provides the best view of the palace. Be prepared, however, to battle dozens of fellow tourists attempting to do the same.

Also built in the 9th century, St Mark's Basilica houses the remains of St Mark the Evangelist. The city cathedral was built in the Byzantine style and has a staggering 8,000 square metres (86,000 square feet) of mosaic covering the walls and vaults. A visit to the Basilica has to be on anyone's Venice itinerary, as is a trip to the top of the 99-metre (323-foot) tall Campanile for incredible views of the city.

The square was built at the same time as the Basilica, and was enlarged in the 12th century – rapidly developing into the heart of the city. The square is the biggest open space in Venice, and can be a welcome relief to the at-times claustrophobic nature of the canal city. It may be a tad expensive, but there are few better places in the world to kick back with a proper Italian-style coffee than at one of the cafes surrounding the square.

You'll appreciate having a rest, because there are so many glorious sights to see around the city, and there are no roads or cars in Venice. There are three ways to get around: on foot, via a water bus or on a gondola. The city is incredibly easy to walk around – you could get around the entire city in about half an hour if you got a good stride on. Make sure you have a detailed map if you're walking Venice without a guide, as the 2,650 alleys can get quite boggling! Other than the footbridges, the water bus (or vaporetto) is the best way to cross the canals or travel through the city if you're getting a bit tired or need to go somewhere quickly. These aren't particularly cheap, but they are regular and it's a lovely way to cruise a Venetian canal if you don't fancy shelling out for a gondola.

Having said that, is a trip to Venice truly complete without a ride on a gondola? These long, narrow boats are synonymous with the city, and provide a romantic, fun way to spend 40 minutes, guided and possibly serenaded by a local expert. There are just 400 licensed gondoliers in Venice, and only two or three licenses are given out per year after a rigorous exam process, so you know you are getting the very best that Venice has to offer. It's a beautiful, unique way to see a city, and an ideal way to have a break from the hustle and bustle of the streets.

The city is a work of art in itself, but if you are in the mood for even more, the Peggy Guggenheim Museum should be an essential part of your trip. Situated in Guggenheim's old house, there are dozens of pieces of Italian and American artwork, as well as new exhibits that have earned this museum global accolades. And if you think you recognise the name, Peggy Guggenheim is the niece of Solomon Guggenheim, who gave his name to the equally famous art gallery in New York. Be sure to visit before it does.

Useful sites
www.veneziaunica.it/en/content/visit-venice-0
www.visit-venice-italy.com/address-tourist-board-venice-italy.htm
venice-tourism.com/en

Venice Carnival is 18 incredible days of balls, parades and fabulous masks

VENICE CARNIVAL

Although Venice is at its most visually stunning in the summer, February to March is carnival season. The carnival takes place in the build up to Lent, meaning that the city is crammed with delicious food and drink to be consumed before the start of the fast. The carnival kicks off with the Flight of the Angel – as the previous year's Mary Carnival winner 'flies' across St Mark's Square. The Venetians really know how to celebrate, with traditional masked galas, parades and regattas along the canals. Venice celebrates its history and heritage in spectacular style, with masquerade balls providing a throwback to the time masks were banned in Venice. The entire city comes out to celebrate. Being such a small city with such a worldwide reputation, Venice can be pretty full, and the addition of thousands of revellers has the city bursting at the seams, but it's an incredible experience not to be missed.

The Rialto Bridge has been a crucial site for locals and tourists for centuries – both functional and beautiful

SOUTH

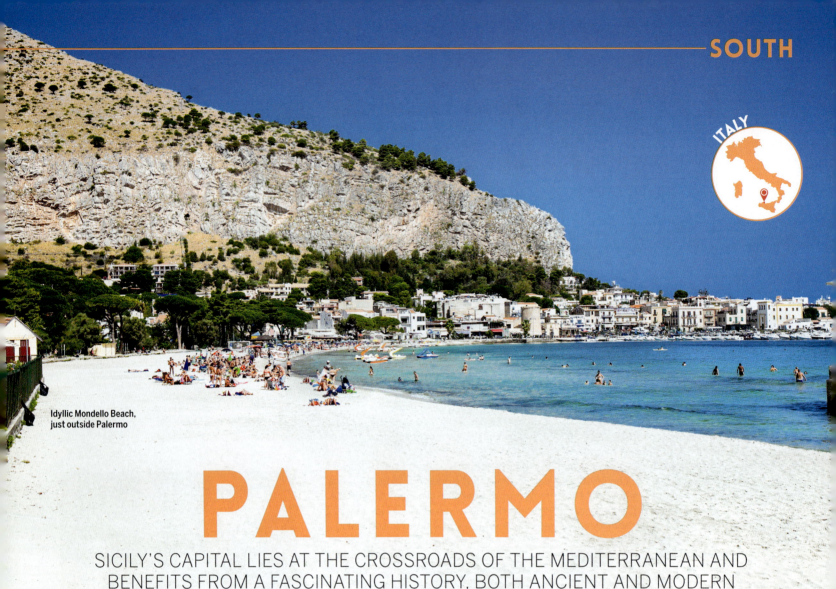

Idyllic Mondello Beach, just outside Palermo

PALERMO

SICILY'S CAPITAL LIES AT THE CROSSROADS OF THE MEDITERRANEAN AND BENEFITS FROM A FASCINATING HISTORY, BOTH ANCIENT AND MODERN

Palermo is the capital of Sicily. It has a population of around 850,000 people and is the cultural and financial centre of the island. It tends to fall under the radar as a city destination because of its island location and beachy/summer holiday vibe, but it's a fascinating place to visit for its incredible history, identity and culture. And anyway, who says you can't combine a beach break with a city break?

Firstly, let's go back in time. A long way. Palermo has a long and fascinating history; in fact, human settlements have been dated as early as 8000 BCE. For visitors now, there are 12 UNESCO sites and a whopping 230 ancient churches to visit, but don't worry, we won't recommend you try and fit them all in. Instead, here's a summary of our top picks.

Palermo Cathedral is listed as a UNESCO World Heritage Site due to its Western, Byzantine and Islamic influences and you can see the blend of Moorish, Catalan and Gothic in the architecture. An entry ticket gets you access to underground rooms, the crypt, treasury, royal tombs and the rooftop, which offers a great view of the city.

We recommend a visit to the contrasting churches of the glitzy 12th century La Martorana – displaying a Baroque front, a Romanesque bell tower and a Byzantine dome – and San Cataldo, its shy and modest neighbour of similar age. Plain on the outside, its mosaic floor is a treat. Mosaics also abound in the pretty Palatine Chapel, built in 804 CE and boasting bright depictions from the bible in precious stone and gold leaf, and marble-inlaid walls. For our final church stop, we're going even further back in time, to the sixth century no less to view the red domes of San Giovanni degli Eremiti.

There's way more to see in Palermo than churches, and it's an eclectic itinerary that ranges from the memorable Capuchin Catacombs, where over 8,000 mummified bodies hang from the walls, to the Teatro Massimo, the third largest opera theatre in Europe and recognisable from *The Godfather III* and back to the Orto Botanico, a 200-year-old botanical garden of citrus trees, tropical plants, herbarium, and glass greenhouses.

And of course, let's not forget the food. Like the rest of the city, Palermo's cuisine is borne from its multicultural roots. Moorish has had a big influence on the food here, seafood is huge, the street markets of Ballaro, Capo, Vucciria and Borgo Vecchio are a great pull to visitors and locals alike and the street food is said to be the best in Europe. In terms of eating out,

Essential information

Cannoli are tubes of fried pastry filled with a sweet ricotta-based creamy filling. They go brilliantly with an al-fresco coffee.

Best time to visit Spring and early summer
Currency € · Euro
Time zone UTC+1

there's a plethora of choice whether you want to eat fancy, or pick up a feast from a no-frills café, grab a pizza or a pastry (it's the home of the cannoli) on the way to the Mondello Beach.

Useful sites
palermocitypass.com
visitsicily.info
wearepalermo.com

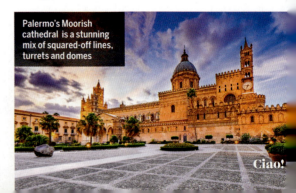

Palermo's Moorish cathedral is a stunning mix of squared-off lines, turrets and domes

SOUTH

SEVILLE

FILLED TO THE BRIM WITH HISTORY, CULTURE AND PASSIONATE LOCALS, YOU'LL DEFINITELY FEEL THE HEAT IN THIS FIERY SPANISH CITY

Occupied by Romans, Muslims and Castilians over the years, you'd think Seville lacked a distinct culture of its own. But while it's certainly been influenced by its inhabitants, Seville retains a fiercely independent spirit and Andalusian personality. Walking through the narrow, shady streets of its Old Town, you'll see colourful flamenco dresses fanning elegantly out of shops, and gazpacho soup served from every tapas bar in sight.

When you emerge from these labyrinthine streets, you may be greeted by a great square, with the Royal Alcázar on one side and Seville's mighty cathedral on the other. You'll want to allow at least half a day to explore the Alcázar, for it is actually three palaces (a Christian one, a Muslim one and a military one). The perfectly symmetrical gardens are arguably the highlight of your visit, so sit down for a cool drink in the cafe and take in the gorgeous aroma of the fruit trees. You can then cross the square to go inside the elaborate cathedral, where some of Spain's most famous figures are buried. Go up La Giralda, an old minaret-turned-bell tower that stands over 100 metres (328 feet) tall.

If you want to explore Seville's more modern side, head south of the city centre to the huge Parque de María Luisa. Whizz round on a bike as you explore its sprawling greenery, perhaps stopping for a picnic under the trees. Inside the park, you'll find the incredible Plaza de España – a grand courtyard and palatial building, constructed for the 1929 World's Fair. It's the perfect setting for a stunning Instagram shot, and you'll find other pretty pavilions dating back from the Fair in the area too. The former Royal Tobacco Factory in the grounds of Seville University is also worth a look, where you'll learn all about Seville's fascinating working-class history.

Head back into the Old Town to clamber up the Metropol Parasol, an interesting sculpture which seems to resemble a wave washing over the city. Built in 2011, it claims to be the largest wooden structure in the world – but it's the sight from the top that makes it stand out. A pathway winds up and down the structure's roof, offering a complete 360-degree panoramic view of Seville's Old Town. It's best visited towards the evening, when the city starts coming to life again after the daily siesta.

As the Sun sets, cross the Guadalquivir River to the Triana district, the home of authentic Sevillan life. Bullfighters, flamenco singers, Spanish dancers and gitanos (Roma people) once called its streets home, and the vibrant nightlife and character of this neighbourhood that you can still experience today are their legacy. It's the perfect place to sip a glass of sherry and round off your city break in Seville.

Useful sites
www.seville-traveller.com
www.visitasevilla.es/en
www.andalucia.com/cities/sevilla.htm

Essential information

Summers in Seville are some of the hottest in Europe, so be prepared for a long, lazy siesta in the mid-afternoon.

Best time to visit April/May, for the Feria (Spring Fair)
Currency € · Euro
Time zone UTC+1

"You'll see colourful flamenco dresses fanning elegantly out of shop"

The Plaza de España in María Luisa Park is a vast construction, built for the 1929 World's Fair

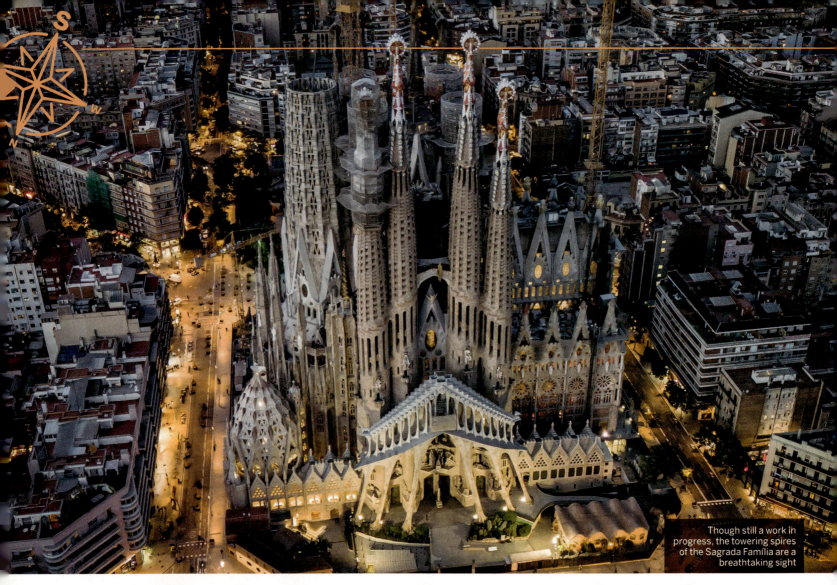

Though still a work in progress, the towering spires of the Sagrada Família are a breathtaking sight

BARCELONA

BARCELONA IS A CITY OF FAMILIAR SIGHTS WHERE THE INFLUENCE OF ONE MAN RISES HIGH

Barcelona has existed as a city for more than 2,000 years, in which time it has accumulated a wealth of staggeringly beautiful buildings, monuments, museums and unmissable sights.

One of the first things on your list of things to see and do in Barcelona has to be the enormously impressive Sagrada Família. This iconic basilica was designed by renowned Catalan artist Antoni Gaudí in the 1880s, but astonishingly is still under construction. Due to the firing of the original architect, Gaudí's untimely death, wars and bureaucratic red tape, the church isn't due to be completed until 2026, but it is still incredible to see the collection of spires soaring into the sky, high above the city. There is a museum within the basilica to explore, but the Sagrada Família is an unmissable part of Barcelona's story, both inside and out, with a fascinating history to boot.

However, if you like your cathedrals a little more complete, Barrio Gotico is your best destination. This charming medieval district is home to a number of essential Barcelona sights, the most iconic of which is the Catedral de la Santa Creu. This stunning creation was started in the late-13th century and completed in the 15th, meaning it has been a Barcelona landmark for well over 600 years. The cathedral has Gothic and Roman features and is certainly worth a visit. After your trip around the cathedral, take some time to explore the rest of the area, as it is full of everything from markets to historic monuments.

Another essential sight is the Montjuïc Castle, which has stood since the mid-17th century at the top of Montjuïc Mountain. This castle retains many of the original features and battlements, proving to be both an educational and fascinating exploration through Spain's military history. It's a good 173 metres (568 feet) above sea level so, if you can face the steep climb, you'll be rewarded with wonderful views over the city and the Balearic Sea.

Another chance to enjoy Barcelona from the sky can be found at the Mirador de Colom. This statue, which has stood for 130 years, commemorates Christopher Columbus's decision to dock at Barcelona port following his successful journey to America, and shows the famed explorer holding a map and pointing the way. You can take a lift 60 metres (200 feet) up inside the column for panoramic views of the city, taking in the cathedral, the Montjuïc Castle and Collserola Natural Park. The Mirador truly is

Essential information

There are numerous multi-day travelcard options to take advantage of in Barcelona.

Best time to visit May-June
Currency € · Euro
Time zone UTC+1

Hola!

SOUTH

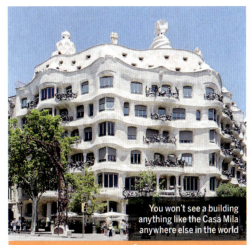

You won't see a building anything like the Casa Mila anywhere else in the world

GAUDÍ CITY

We have already learned a lot about Gaudí's most famous piece of work in Barcelona – the Sagrada Família – but his influence stretches far and wide across the city. The Casa Mila is one of the most eye-catching and polarising buildings in the world. As with the Sagrada Família, the building of this enormous family home was beset with difficulties, which resulted in its unique appearance. It's now open to the public as an activity centre and museum and has to be seen from all angles to truly get an understanding of why this UNESCO Heritage Site is both loved and hated in equal measure. More successful was Park Güell – a Gaudí-designed residential park that was commissioned by Barcelona-born businessman Eusebi Güell in the early part of the 20th century. The park is now public property but retains all the quirky, mind-boggling designs that Gaudí became renowned for.

a breathtaking sight, whether you're looking at it or looking out from it.

The Mirador is situated on La Rambla, one of Barcelona's main boulevards that sits at the very centre of the city. It's a popular artery from which to branch out and explore other areas of Barcelona. One such area is the similarly named Rambla de Catalunya, which is much quieter and is lined with shops and restaurants. Another place for you to get your shopping fix is La Boqueria Market. Barcelona is one of the foodie capitals of the continent and this is where the city shows off its most glorious array of fresh vegetables, meats, seafood and fruit. If you want to enjoy some local produce as well as some of the best tapas Barcelona has to offer, then La Boqueria, which calls itself the world's best market, is certainly the place to go.

Not only is it famous for its architecture and food, but Barcelona also has a global reputation for sport. FC Barcelona is one of the world's most successful football teams, and taking in a match or tour of the iconic Camp Nou stadium is essential for any self-respecting football fan. Barcelona also played host to the 1992 Olympics, so a tour of the Olympic Stadium is a fascinating experience for anyone intrigued to see the place where Great Britain's Linford Christie famously won 100-metre sprint gold.

Kids are also well catered for in Barcelona, with the Tibidabo Amusement Park an incredibly fun day out for kids and adults of all ages. The park is packed with entertaining rides, stalls and activities that you could comfortably spend an entire day enjoying. It is much more reasonably priced than many British amusement parks, so could be a chance for a kid-focused day that won't cost the Earth.

Barcelona offers so much as a travel destination and can be comfortably seen in a long weekend or a wonderful week away, enjoying the city sights as well as the beaches that Spain is so famous for.

Barcelona is a truly cosmopolitan city. It has the charm and history of an ancient city, while having the modern qualities that make it the ideal travel destination for families, couples or single travellers looking to soak up the Sun, culture, food and history of one of Europe's oldest and most famous cities.

Useful sites
www.barcelonaturisme.com/wv3/en/
www.barcelona.com
www.barcelonapass.com

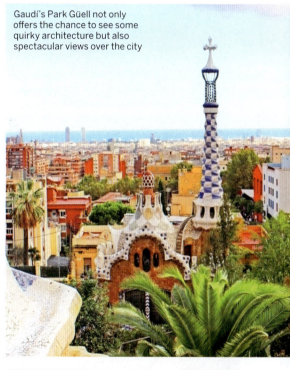

Gaudí's Park Güell not only offers the chance to see some quirky architecture but also spectacular views over the city

A trip to Barcelona has to include a visit to one of the world's most iconic sports stadiums, Camp Nou

Barcelona's Barrio Gotico (Gothic Quarter) is famous for its labyrinth of narrow streets

VALENCIA

DISCOVER THE COASTAL CITY FAMED FOR ITS ORANGES WHERE THE RIVER TURIA MEETS THE FISH-FILLED WATERS OF THE MEDITERRANEAN SEA

As Spain's third-largest city, Valencia exudes vivacity with its glorious scenery, distinctive flavours and true regional identity. Home to one of Europe's busiest ports, this vibrant and somewhat futuristic city boasts a growing cultural scene, but it is the city's food and outlook on the environment that really sets it apart from the rest of the country.

The city benefits from 2 million square metres of gardens and approximately 20 kilometres of outstanding golden beaches. One of the largest urban parks in the country are the Turia Gardens, with routes stretching over ten kilometres (six miles). It is a fabulous spot to enjoy a huge variety of flora while sipping a coffee and sampling a 'farton', a local sweet pastry dusted in sugar. The gardens are connected to the famous City of Arts and Sciences and the Parque de la Cabecera, which is located in the bed of the Turia River.

The park is split into sections, including the Mediterranean riverside woodland, the mountain viewpoint and the Biopark, which is the biggest zoological park in the city and home to free-roaming animals. Also featuring a bar and an open-air auditorium, it's just one of many great locations for a picnic, which you can pick up at the Mercat Central, Europe's largest undercover market. Its impressive arts deco facade houses an incredible 400 stalls selling fresh produce from both land and sea. Here you can shop for cured meats, cheeses, seasonal vegetables and even sea urchins for those feeling adventurous.

When the time comes for a break from touring Valencia's streets, why not enjoy a horchata inside one of the 'horchaterias' that surround the market. This creamy concoction is made from tigernuts ('chufas'), water and sugar and is perfectly refreshing on a summer's day. Tigernuts were originally brought to the city by the Egyptians and are now grown outside its perimeters along with persimmons, almonds, olives, cherries and citrus fruits. Speaking of farming, agricultural tours can be arranged for those wanting to explore outside the city.

If time permits, take a trip to L'Albufera Natural Park. Once at the park you can travel around by foot, bicycle or on an albuferenc, a type of handcrafted boat that can be found at the ports in El Palmar, Sollana, Silla and Catarroja. The 40-minute journey is well worth the effort for nature – and particularly bird – lovers, as L'Albuferas freshwater lagoon is home to 300 different bird species, including flamingos and waterfowl.

This urban oasis is surrounded by woods and paddyfields of Valencian rice; no surprise given that paella hails from the city. Originally a simple, hearty meal prepared for and by farmers and labourers, who would gather around the pan to eat, paella would be made using seasonal vegetables, rice, butter beans, saffron, rabbit and even snails. The best spot for enjoying paella can be found at Malvarrosa city beach, where the dish is cooked over a wood fire, for a smoky flavour. Pair this with a jug of 'Aqua de Valencia' (made from the juice of the city's famous oranges, gin, vodka and cava) or one of the city's splendid regional wines for a truly authentic Valencian meal. Salud!

Useful sites
visitvalencia.com/en/what-to-see-valencia/must-sees
parquesnaturales.gva.es/es/web/pn-l-albufera
www.valenbisi.es/en/home

From the 14th to the 18th century, the silk trade was Valencia's life blood. The Silk Exchange, a striking building replete with late Gothic columns, stands testament to this crucial industry

Essential information

🇪🇸 Be sure to pay a visit to some of the architecturally stunning metro stations of the city, including the Alameda and Colón stations.

Best time to visit During Las Fallas, one of the craziest festivals on Earth. It's usually held during March, but check for specific dates.

Currency € · Euro

Time zone UTC+1

SOUTH

PALMA

YES, IT'S SUN-BAKED AND BEACH-EDGED, BUT PALMA DE MALLORCA HAS A WEALTH OF HISTORY THAT MAY SURPRISE YOU

Palma de Mallorca is the kind of place, in the depths of winter, you remember with a particular yearning. "Oh, take me back there!", you might moan to yourself as another fog-filled day draws to a close and you can barely believe that honey-coloured stone and those crystal-clear waters exist.

The city radiates out from the magnificent cathedral in the middle, which defines its silhouette; La Seu is a sandstone Gothic masterpiece that took 400 years to build and counts Gaudi among its more recent renovators. Alongside the cathedral in terms of iconic monuments is the Arab Baths, discovered only 100 years ago but dating back as far as the 10th or 12th century. It's a small place but fascinating to see the columns reclaimed from different periods of ancient history.

In fact, fragments of the past are everywhere to be found in Palma, not least of which is in the Jewish Quarter, the Call Maior, a section of the city with its own walls and entrances. And also at Bellver Castle which, although it sounds like a National Trust property in Devon, is actually one of only a handful of circular castles in Europe. In the final stop on this old-buildings trail, there's the Royal Palace of La Almudaina, a mix of Roman castle and Muslim alcazar dating from the late 1200s. A quiver in its armoury is the fact you get fantastic views over Mallorca from its elevated location.

Back down by the sea, there's a fantastic promenade and cyclable path which, if you go east, takes you to the little port of Portixol. It's only ten minutes on two wheels so perfectly possible for a quiet lunch and a dip in the sea.

Back in the city, it's time to don an artist's smock. Hit up Es Baluard Museum of Modern and Contemporary Art, where the big-name quota is high with the likes of Picasso and Miró among 500 represented artists. Seek out the Fundacio Joan March Museum on Calle Sant Miquel, which is dedicated to the eponymous Catalan painter and concentrates on Spanish works from the 20th century including Salvador Dali. The Fundació Pilar i Joan Miró, set up by Miró and his wife shortly before he died, on the hill outside town, allows visitors to see his studios and provides another excellent view of the city's rooftops and sea beyond.

Other top tips for a stay in Mallorca centre largely around eating: 1) Don't miss Palma's food markets in the shape of El Mercat de Santa Catalina, Mercat de l'Olivar and Mercat 1930. 2) Start your day with a café con leche and a pan con tomate (this is another thing you'll be dreaming of on a dreary winter's day at home: a mix of fresh tomato and olive oil spread on toast) or try an ensaimada, a traditional Mallorcan spiral-shaped sweet pastry. 3) Tapas. As you'd expect it's everywhere and you can't really go wrong. One thing to note is that if you're in town on a Tuesday, get yourself along to Gerreria in the old town for Ruta Martiana, essentially a bar crawl with tapas designed to get people out on the quietest evening of the week.

Useful sites
catedraldemallorca.org
illesbalears.travel
visitpalma.com/en

Essential information

While tapas are small portions, a pintxo is smaller still. A pintxo is often held on a toothpick, which gives you an idea of size.

Best time to visit Spring, summer, autumn
Currency € · Euro
Time zone UTC+1

La Seu, Palma's stunning sandstone Gothic cathedral, dominates the seafront

SAN SEBASTIÁN

KNOWN FOR ITS MICHELIN-STARRED FOOD SCENE, THIS POPULAR BASQUE PORT IS A GASTRONOMIC NIRVANA, WITH A DISH TO PLEASE EVERY PALATE

Known to the locals as Donostia (Basque for 'Saint Sebastian'), the city of San Sebastián has become famous among food lovers for its pintxo bars, gourmet food shops and local produce markets, not to mention its numerous highly acclaimed restaurants, three of which hold the highest award of three Michelin stars.

Located on the coast of the Bay of Biscay, this picturesque port benefits from some of the freshest fish and seafood available. San Sebastián lives and breathes food, and fresh, high-quality fare is what it's all about. Local and seasonal produce are always the dish of the day, with many of the top restaurants sourcing their produce from the city's markets, making them a good place to start when exploring.

At the La Bretxa market you can expect to find only the freshest vegetables, with stalls piled high with asparagus, artichokes, all manner of beans and guindilla peppers. Inside and underground are the fish and meat sections, stocked to the gill with hake, turbot, chistorra sausage and other delicacies.

The markets are a great place to buy picnic items to take to the La Concha beach, where you will be greeted by a mile of glorious golden sand and a promenade that provides views of the Miramar Palace, built for the Spanish royal family in the late 19th century.

Given the mountainous nature of the region and the presence of the Ebro Valley, it's no surprise that hiking is hugely popular in the area, with many trail options to the top of the Monte Urgull alongside coastal and woodland routes. Alternatively, you can hop aboard the red funicular (built in 1912) and take a ride to the top of Monte Igueldo to admire the spectacular views of Monte Urgull, the old town, beach and Santa Clara Island. There is even a vintage fairground at the top, with a haunted house for those feeling brave!

With food being high on the agenda, digging into the local cuisine is a mouthwatering necessity. We are all familiar with tapas, but in the Basque region they have their own style known as pintxos. Pintxos bars all serve tasty morsels of cheese, meats, fish and croquettes laid on top of small pieces of bread to accompany your beverages. This region of Spain produces a delicious, dry, lightly sparkling wine called Txakoli that happens to pair very well with pintxos.

The majority of the bars are located in the old town, each with its own set of specialities. Take a wander through the alleyways of the Parte Vieja and discover your favourite spots, finishing the evening with an artisanal ice cream and a stroll along the boulevard.

In contrast to the narrow streets of the old town is the Gros neighbourhood, an area that moves to a slightly younger, more dynamic beat. With the La Zurriola surf beach at its helm and numerous quirky shops, funky cafes and of course yet more pintxos bars, it's a lively place to head to for a night out.

Useful sites
motorasdelaisla.com/en/
guide.michelin.com/us/en/pais-vasco/es-donostia-san-sebastian/restaurants
sansebastianpintxos.com/en/

A breathtaking view of San Sebastián, with its golden La Concha beach, Santa Clara Island and mountainous valleys in the distance

Essential information

Visit Santa Clara Island with Motoras de la Isla, a family company that has sailed there for over 80 years.

Best time to visit June to Sept

Currency € · Euro

Time zone UTC+1

SOUTH

The Plaza de Cibeles, with its neo-classical marble statues and fountains, has become a symbol for the city of Madrid

Essential information

Spain's metro is easy to use and navigate, so take advantage of it when travelling.

Best time to visit March to May for balmier weather

Currency € · Euro

Time zone UTC+1

MADRID

SPAIN'S CAPITAL IS CAPTIVATING THANKS TO ITS BROAD ARTISTIC SPECTRUM

Stepping out into the crowded streets of Madrid, you'll be amazed to see that the city is a rich tapestry of European art. One of the most prominent buildings in Madrid is its Royal Palace. While it no longer houses Spain's royal family, it is still their official residence. The building itself, one of 12 palaces in the region, was inspired by sketches made by the artist Bernini for Paris's most famous museum – the Louvre.

Inside the palace walls you will find an impressive armoury and painting gallery, featuring artistic gems from Luis de Morales, Juan de Flandes, Diego Velázquez and Joaquín Sorolla. Not far away the Liria Palace has recently opened its doors to the public. The palace's library is home to one of the first Spanish translations of the Old Testament and a collection of Christopher Columbus' letters.

The ultimate foodie experience in this city can be found at Sobrino de Botín. Found on Calle de Cuchilleros, this restaurant holds the title of the world's oldest restaurant according to the Guinness World Records. Opened in 1725, it still features a stunning 16th-century dining area. This little hideaway and its roast suckling pig was favoured by the literary godfather Ernest Hemingway (and mentioned in his book *The Sun Also Rises*) during his travels around the peninsular. The artist Francisco Goya, considered to be Spain's most important artist throughout the 18th and 19th centuries, worked in the cafe as a waiter while waiting to get accepted into the Royal Academy of Fine Arts.

A short walk away is the beautiful Parque del Oeste and arguably its most fascinating monument – the Templo de Debod. The Egyptian structure, more than 2,200 years old, is dedicated to the gods Amon and Isis and was sent brick by brick as a thank you to Spain from the Egyptian government in 1968 for helping to preserve their monuments, which were being threatened by the rising reservoir of the Aswan Dam. Another fascinating thread to Madrid's rich tapestry is located in central Madrid: the Museo Nacional del Prado. This building is the Spanish national art museum, which houses stunning Spanish Romanesque murals and Gothic altarpieces, as well as classical and Renaissance sculptures.

On a sleepy Sunday morning, the area of Calle de la Ribera de Curtidores comes alive after 7am, when the street unfolds its five-centuries-old market, which offers a taste of the bustling Madrid unlike any other.

Useful sites
www.esmadrid.com/en
www.turismomadrid.es/en
www.spain.info/en

Formerly Casa Botin, the world's oldest restaurant, Sobrino de Botín was opened in 1725 and is famous for its suckling pig

Madrid's Gran Vía is the place to head if you're looking for some retail therapy

The famous Guggenheim Museum is an architectural marvel, drawing in the crowds to the world of contemporary art

BILBAO

SET YOUR SAT NAV TO BILBAO, AND EXPERIENCE NORTHERN SPAIN'S BEAUTIFUL AND SCENIC BASQUE COUNTRY BEFORE SETTING FOOT IN A CITY OF ART AND CULTURE

Named European City of the Year 2018, Bilbao is a city of development and change, transforming itself from an industrial port city exporting ironworks to a tourist hotspot in the Basque Country.

Take one look at the Guggenheim Museum and you'll witness how, in the 1990s, Bilbao's tourism changed forever. The museum of modern and contemporary art has put Bilbao back on the global map, featuring art from the 20th century to modern day, inside an incredible building that stands out in the city.

The medieval Casco Viejo, also known as Seven Streets because of its parallel roads, forms the Old Quarter. Sights include the grand Santiago Cathedral, displaying a mix of architectural styles, from its Gothic spire to the 15th-century cloister. While visiting Casco Viejo, don't miss the beautiful Teatro Arriaga, a venue for performing arts and concerts.

Semana Grande, or Aste Nagusia, is a nine-day festival held every August. It celebrates the Basque culture while honouring the Virgen de Begoña. Celebrate in one of the street concerts, firework displays, parades, food fights and even bullfights. With more than 100,000 people attending the event, there's no better way to get stuck into the Basque culture.

Your journey to Bilbao should include a stop at the Santander train station. Situated along the estuary, this is an ideal spot to sample scrummy Basque cider. And you can't visit Bilbao without eating the local speciality, pintxos. These little tapas-style snacks form the backbone of Basque cuisine, and there are plenty of places to grab a bite while exploring the city's alleyways. Take a stroll over the Zubizuri footbridge, cross the Nervión river and walk southwards to where you can find the Teatro Arriaga opera house. Bilbao's continued development and creativity will forever change the future of this hidden European gem.

Useful sites
bilbaoturismo.net
guggenheim-bilbao.eus/en euskoguide.com

Essential information

Siesta happens at around 2pm, with shops closing then reopening three to four hours later.

Best time to visit June to September
Currency € • Euro
Time zone UTC+2

SOUTH

Essential information

Port's EU-protected status means only Douro Valley wine can be called Port – so stock up!

Best time to visit June for weather and festivals

Currency € · Euro

Time zone UTC

Porto's colourful Old Town lines the city's Douro River

PORTO

ENJOY THE ULTIMATE CHEESE AND WINE NIGHT AT THE HOME OF PORT AND THE CHEESE CASTLE

Porto is Portugal's second city, located 315 kilometres (200 miles) north of the capital, Lisbon. Home to one of the country's most successful football teams, Porto is also known as the city that gave the world Port wine – the ultimate after-dinner tipple.

Portugal has been exporting wine since the 12th century, with the first reference to Port appearing in 1678. The finest climate and terrain for growing wine grapes was in the lands around the Douro River, the waterway that forms part of the border between Portugal and Spain. However, the wine had to be transported down the river and fortified with brandy to keep it from spoiling. Thus, Port wine was created. Now, some 340 years later, you can recreate the journey of those intrepid seekers of great grapes with your very own trip along the Douro River, taking in the sights, smells and, of course, tastes of the wine villages that line the banks of the river.

However, Porto isn't all about the wine. Cheese is the perfect partner, and cheese is the basis for two of Porto's must-dos. Firstly, there is the Castelo do Queijo, or Castle of Cheese. This 17th-century fortress guards Porto from Atlantic invaders and is officially known as Forte de São Francisco Xavier, but is know by its nickname due to the cheese-shaped outcrop of rock it sits upon. Geology notwithstanding, the castle is well worth a visit. Its impressive yet quirky design, centuries-old cannons and view over the ocean make it a wonderful spot for some family sightseeing.

If a stroll around a historical castle has whetted your appetite, why not try a Francesinha, a culinary delight unique to Porto. This hefty meal comprises pork, smoked sausage, bacon, beefsteak, fried egg and a rich cheese sauce, often served with chips. Not the healthiest, but it's worth tucking into this local speciality. Porto's coastal location also makes it a prime place for seafood – Bolhão market is a must if you're there on a self-catering break.

The bridges in Porto are both functional and beautiful. The Maria Pia railway bridge was designed by none other than Gustave Eiffel, while it's recommended you take a wander across the Dom Luís I bridge, which is its equal in breathtaking beauty and views.

The stunning Porto Library also has to feature on your trip as it is an incredible sight, as are the Igreja do Carmo and Carmelitas – churches adorned with beautiful blue, locally made tiles.

Porto is a bustling, exciting city, so fill your boots with its historical and culinary delights.

Useful sites
www.discoveroporto.com/envisitgreece.gr/
en/www.visitporto.travel/Visitar/Paginas/
Default.aspx
www.porto-north-portugal.com/index.html

The Baroque Igreja do Carmo is decorated with beautiful azulejo tiles

The Castelo de São Jorge sits proudly on a hill overlooking the colourful city

Essential information

🇵🇹 Order a pastéis de nata (or Portuguese custard tart) in the morning or evening.

Best time to visit Best weather in March-May or September-October

Currency € · Euro

Time zone UTC

Olá!

SOUTH

LISBON

VISIT THE CITY THAT BRINGS FLAVOURS OF PARIS AND RIO TO THE IBERIAN PENINSULA

Lisbon is Portugal's capital and largest city in terms of population by some distance. More than twice as many people live there than live in the second-largest city, Porto, and it is also one of the most-visited. Its history can be traced back an astonishing 3,000 years, making it one of the world's oldest cities, and, as such, is packed with icons of the country's illustrious sailing history, beautiful architecture as well as historic markets.

One of the oldest landmarks in the city is the Castelo de São Jorge. It was built in the 11th century by the ruling Moors to defend the city against invading forces, before turning into the seat of the King of Portugal. The castle stands high on a hilltop, providing gorgeous views over the city in one direction and the mouth of the Tagus River in the other. Partially ruined by an earthquake in 1755, the castle was restored in the 1940s. Unfortunately for history buffs, it may not be an entirely faithful recreation, but it has made for a beautiful and safe structure to wander around and admire.

The Portuguese global expansion began in the 1400s and took them as far afield as Brazil in South America, Mozambique in Africa and Goa in Asia. Two relics of this prosperous era are the Mosteiro dos Jerónimos and the Torre de Belém – both very much worth a visit. Jerónimos took well over 100 years to complete, having been started in 1501, and was built to commemorate one of Portugal's most famed sailors, Vasco da Gama. The UNESCO World Heritage Site is a Portuguese Gothic-style monastery, while the adjoining Church of Santa Maria is the final resting place of da Gama. Near to Jerónimos is the Tower of Belém. Originally built as a waterfront defence against invading forces, Belém has also been a lighthouse, but now exists as one of the country's most popular tourist attractions. Beware though – only 150 people are allowed in the tower at a time, so get there early or prepare for a long queue. One thing not to miss is the statue carving of a rhinoceros on the western facade, commemorating the arrival of a rhino from India in the 1500s.

Lisbon's status as a truly global city can be seen in two iconic landmarks. The statue of Christ the Redeemer stands high above the city of Rio de Janeiro, but Lisbon hosts the European equivalent. Cristo Rei was inaugurated 30 years after Christ the Redeemer on the Tejo Estuary in 1959, and stands just over 100 metres (330 feet) – a symbol of religious gratitude for Portugal avoiding the worst of World War II.

The other global influence is a little closer to home, however. The Elevador de Santa Justa is a staggeringly beautiful wrought-iron lift that takes tourists 45 metres (147 feet) above ground level, providing some of the most spectacular views of the city, as well as a link to the beautiful Largo do Carmo square. Construction started in 1900, having been designed by Lisbon native Raoul Mesnier de Ponsard – a student of the great Gustave Eiffel, who is better known for another fairly iconic wrought-iron structure.

A short walk from the lift is an example of Lisbon's rich religious history. Lisbon Cathedral is the city's oldest and most impressive church, having been built in the 12th century. As with the Castelo de São Jorge, the cathedral was damaged in the 1755 earthquake, but has also been beautifully restored and is a must-see during a visit to the city.

For shopaholics, the Feira da Ladra flea market is the perfect place to stroll around and pick up a bargain or two. The market is in place on Tuesdays and Saturdays, offering everything from clothes to furniture.

If you're feeling peckish, the Bairro do Avillez is a gorgeous complex of restaurants. Depending on your mood and taste, you can choose to eat in the traditional Taberna, spacious, seafood-heavy Páteo or artisan grocer A Mercearia.

Sports fans can visit the Estádio José Alvalade stadium, where the tour includes a visit to the World of Sporting museum, which has a section devoted to one of their most famous exports – Cristiano Ronaldo.

Lisbon is a wonderful, historic city that is bursting at the seams with cultural, religious, shopping and foodie experiences. The main sights can be seen comfortably in a long weekend, but its temperate climate and size means that a week won't feel too long either. Lisbon offers something for pretty much every traveller, so you'd wonder why all those sailors ever wanted to leave these shores.

Useful sites
www.visitlisboa.com/en/p/why-lisbon
www.castelodesaojorge.pt/en/ porto-north-
www.lisbon.net

A Portuguese custard tart with coffee is an essential part of any stay in Lisbon

Enjoy the beauty and serenity of the Praia da Adraga beach deep in the Sintra-Cascais Natural Park

LISBON'S A BEACH

Walking the landmarks of a sunny city can be hot and tiring work, so you may want a day or two relaxing on a beach. Lisbon itself, despite being on the banks of a river, doesn't have any beaches, but there are some stunning sandy vistas a short journey away. Most of the best beaches can be found in the Cascais area, which can be reached by public transport or hire car within about half an hour. These beaches lie on the edge of the Atlantic Ocean, many providing superb opportunities for surfing. Further afield is the Praia da Adraga, a wildly wonderful beach located in the Sintra-Cascais Natural Park, where you can look out over the ocean from 100m (330ft) high cliffs. In order to have a permanent reminder of your visit, ask for a diploma that proves you were at the westernmost point of Europe.

Olá!

ATHENS

GREECE'S ANCIENT CAPITAL IS FULL OF LIFE, PASSION AND CHARACTER JUST ASK THE LOCALS

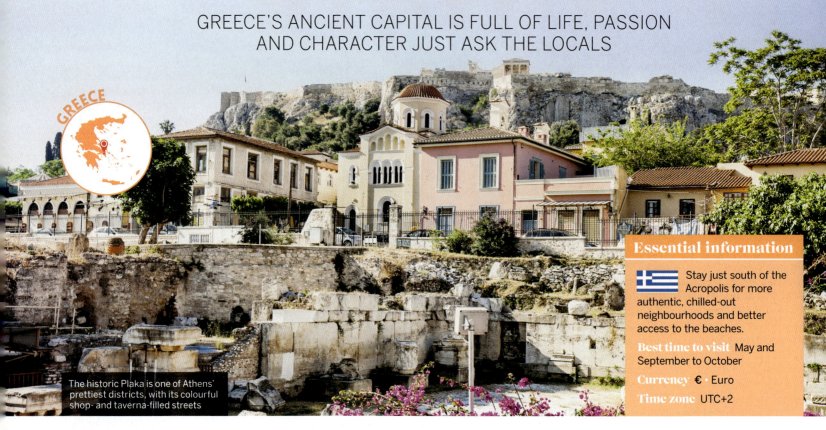

The historic Plaka is one of Athens' prettiest districts, with its colourful shop- and taverna-filled streets

Essential information

Stay just south of the Acropolis for more authentic, chilled-out neighbourhoods and better access to the beaches.

Best time to visit May and September to October

Currency € · Euro

Time zone UTC+2

The southernmost capital on Europe's mainland Western civilisation, but it's also making waves in the modern world. Athens is a vibrant place, where graffiti meets Greek gods, and you'll want to check out all it has to offer. Athens' most iconic sight is its ancient Acropolis, complete with the Parthenon temple, Odeon of Herodes Atticus, and many more ruins. Start at the southern entrance and check out the remains of the ancient city as you work your way up the Acropolis. Pass under the mighty Propylaea and you'll be greeted with a breathtaking view of the marble Parthenon. From the top, admire the views spanning the city and be sure to take lots of photos standing beside the larger-than-life Greek flag. You can continue to get your ancient fix by exploring the Roman Agora, Hadrian's Arch and the windswept Temple of Olympian Zeus at the foot of the Acropolis.

If it's a more modern vibe you're after, just a stone's throw away is Syntagma Square, where the hubbub of modern Athens is in full swing. Check out the Greek parliament building or watch the hustle and bustle of the square from the rooftop bar at the Hotel Grande Bretagne. Walk to Kolonaki to enjoy its fancy shops and cafes, where Greek politicians and intellectuals rub shoulders with tourists. For a breath of fresh air, be sure to visit the National Botanic Gardens and see the cute turtles as they splash about in freshwater ponds.

If you need a break from the Athenian heat, cool off at one of many spots nearby. Lake Vouliagmeni retains a pleasant temperature of around 20 degrees Celsius (68 Fahrenheit) all year, and is a popular destination among the locals. If you're looking for some seaside fun, Glyfada and Vouliagmeni are known for their lively beach bars, which often have swimming pools and dance floors to get you in the party mood – best enjoyed with a cocktail in hand.

As the sun sets over the Acropolis, the city truly comes alive. Watch a (subtitled) movie in one of Athens' quirky outdoor cinemas and mingle with Greek film fans. Later on, join the Greeks for dinner at about 9pm, when the tavernas and restaurants of the Plaka are at their busiest. Check out the many bars of Monastiraki, from high-end hotspots to traditional Greek music halls. Finish your night with a stroll along Dionysiou Areopagitou, and look up at the illuminated Acropolis as the warm wind blows around you. Athens is just as exciting now as it was two millennia ago.

Useful sites

www.thisisathens.org
www.athensguide.com
www.visitgreece.gr/en/main-cities/athens

The Parthenon was built to honour the goddess Athena

In Athens, you're never more than half an hour away from a slice of summer paradise

SOUTH

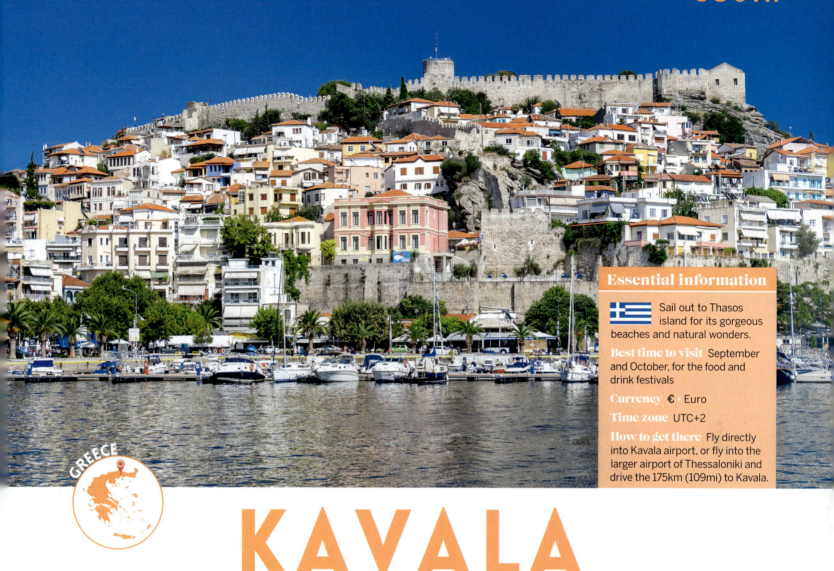

Essential information

🇬🇷 Sail out to Thasos island for its gorgeous beaches and natural wonders.

Best time to visit September and October, for the food and drink festivals

Currency € · Euro

Time zone UTC+2

How to get there Fly directly into Kavala airport, or fly into the larger airport of Thessaloniki and drive the 175km (109mi) to Kavala.

KAVALA

VISIT THE CITY WHERE ANCIENT ROME MEETS ANCIENT GREECE

Northern Greece is an underrated part of this gorgeous country, and Kavala is a great place to start exploring it. Halfway between Thessaloniki and the Turkish border, this hodgepodge city is jam-packed with atmospheric sights, a unique vibe, and absolutely delicious food.

Through the ages, Kavala has been occupied by people from across Europe – the Romans, the Byzantines, the Venetians, the Ottomans and even the Crusaders have all left their mark on the landscape. Kavala's historic heart is its old town, the centrepiece of which is a Byzantine fortress that looks like it comes straight out of a fairytale. With its hilltop vantage point and storybook battlements and turrets, it's a great photo opportunity as well as a fascinating place to visit. You can look out over the city and breathe in the salty sea air, the wind providing welcome relief from the sun.

Travel forward in time to experience the Ottoman side of town. Marvel at the iconic 16th-century aqueduct, which like a vein through the city carried water to the homes, businesses and bathhouses of Ottoman Kavala. Step into the grounds of the colourful Halil Bey Mosque and run your hands over its blue, green and terracotta-painted walls. Inside the main prayer hall you can walk the glass floor to peer over the remains of the Christian church on the site, and go out to the courtyard to explore the well-preserved madrasa (Islamic school).

If the madrasa takes your fancy, you're in luck – amble 170m (558ft) down Ali Mehmet street and you can stay in a luxury hotel that was converted from a theological college. Water was a key tenet of Ottoman design, and the hotel's courtyard is home to an inviting pool. The cistern, meanwhile, has been converted into a cosy, sensual spa.

No matter where you go in Greece, the sea is never too far away, and Kavala sits right on it. You'll find some of the best seafood in town along Erithrou Stavrou promenade, which after dark transforms into a lively nightlife district.

If authenticity is what you're after, however, you can check out the mezedopoleía (Greek tapas restaurants) and ouzo bars in the narrow backstreets located slightly inland. They frequently host live music nights, where you can truly immerse yourself and experience Kavala in its full kefi (fun-filled) spirit.

Greece is renowned across the globe for its beautiful beaches, exciting towns, incredible food and friendly people. Kavala has all that to offer and much more. It really is a wonder why the rest of the world hasn't discovered it yet. Be sure to visit before it does.

Useful sites
visitkavala.gr/en/
visitgreece.gr/en/main_cities/kavala
kavalagreece.gr/en/

"The Byzantine fortress looks like it comes straight out of a fairytale"

The White Tower, for centuries part of the old city walls, houses a museum on Thessaloniki's history and a spectacular view from the roof

Essential information

🇬🇷 Cash is often preferred in Greece, so make sure to always have some on you.

Best time to visit
March to June

Currency € · Euro

Time zone UTC+2

THESSALONIKI

MANY STORIES, ONE HEART: A CITY SLOGAN AS TRUE AS THEY COME

Glittering on the Thermaic Gulf, Thessaloniki is a gem. the White Tower offers the best 360-degree views of the city and waterfront from the roof (helpfully avoiding tourists gatecrashing your photos) for £7 ($8) from April to October, or £3 ($4) in the off-season. A three-day combined ticket is also available for £13 ($16), valid for entry into the White Tower, the Museum of Byzantine Culture, the Archaeological Museum of Thessaloniki, and the Rotunda.

From White Tower Square, the Arabella pirate ship departs regularly for a free 30-minute port cruise – just be aware that you're expected to buy a drink, which is a small price to pay for sailing with a bona fide pirate. Expect to spend £6-£8 ($8-$9) on a beverage, either alcoholic or not. Back on land, a walk along the waterfront will bring you to the six-metre-tall (20 feet) Alexander the Great statue, followed by the Umbrellas of Thessaloniki, like so many dandelion puffs in the wind – visit at sunset to see them glow, or at sunrise if you want to avoid the crowds.

For a bit of local everything, visit Bit Bazar, a mixture of stalls and traditional tavernas offering affordable drinks and mezedes. Alternatively, head to the Kapani Market, rich with local spices, cheese, olives, and freshly caught fish. (The famous Modiano Market reopened in late 2022 after its major restoration.) Afterwards, visit the UNESCO World Heritage Site of the Hagia Sophia church, one of the oldest in the city and famed for its Byzantine art and architecture, and wander through the nearby Louloudadika flower market, easily the most colourful place in the city.

Ano Poli, the Upper Town, is absolutely worth the hike, but make sure you bring a cold drink and a beer to enjoy at the top – it's quite a trek. Walk up from the Roman Forum along narrow cobblestone streets, past hidden gardens and old houses, to Trigonion Tower. Free to enter, you can walk the walls for panoramic views of Thessaloniki. The Heptapyrgion fortress is 0.5 kilometres (0.3 miles) higher up, is also free but distinctly unsettling, particularly the solitary confinement wing. On the way back down through Ano Poli, stop off in a side-street taverna to recover with authentic local food and a glass of ouzo or tsipouro.

Of course, this is Greece, so beaches can't be forgotten. If you rent a car, visit the turquoise waters of the Halkidiki peninsulas, or stay closer to home and take the £6 ($7) water taxi to the white sands of Peraia Beach. Springtime temperatures are absolutely perfect and the crowds are few. If you fancy a day trip further afield, consider taking the bus to Kastoria (three hours; £26 ($31) return) for its stunning lake and the Dragon's Cave, only £5 ($6) to enter. Lastly, if you want to explore Mount Olympus, take the train to Litochoro (57 minutes; £12 ($15) return) as a starting point – from there, you're free to enter the mythical home of the gods.

Useful sites
lpth.gr/indexeg.php
hellenictrain.gr/en
thessalonikitourism.gr/index.php/en

SOUTH

VALLETTA

THIS BUSTLING OUTDOOR MUSEUM OF A CITY IS STEEPED IN HISTORY AND BLESSED WITH AZURE WATERS AND PLENTIFUL SUNSHINE

With a unique charm all of its own, the Maltese capital city of Valletta was built on a peninsula between two natural harbours, with its streets set out in a grid-like formation to allow plenty of sea breeze in during the scorching summer months. Despite being one of Europe's smallest capitals, Valletta packs a huge historical and cultural punch, so much so that the whole city is an officially listed UNESCO World Heritage site.

Sixteenth-century bastion walls envelope a city that over the last few years has undergone a revitalisation, with many historic sites and museums restored to their former glory and the building of new boutique hotels, bars and restaurants bringing fresh life to Valletta's ancient streets. Strait Street is a prime example of how the continent's southernmost capital has changed. Once the city's red light district, it has been transformed into the centre of the nightlife scene, thronging with patrons eating and drinking in the recently constructed bars and restaurants.

As you walk through the narrow side streets, filled with quaint shops and bustling cafes, take time to appreciate the 320 monuments scattered around the city, all of them dedicated to Valletta's illustrious founders. Stop by the tiny row of jewellery shops on St Lucy Street that sell intricate Maltese silver filigree, and if you're feeling peckish a trip to the Victorian covered market of Is-Suq Tal-Belt will soon satisfy your stomach. This food hall has everything you could ask for, from traditional pastizzi (pastries) filled with local cheese and peas to Turkish meze and octopus or sea bass fresh from the Mediterranean. Don't shy away from the local delicacies, though. Halva, capers, figs and jam made from prickly pears can all be picked up here.

Such is the layout of Valletta that whichever sloping street you walk down you will be rewarded with a glistening view of the harbour, a burst of exotic wildflower or a charming piazza in which to sit and enjoy watching the world go by. Nestled on the top of the eastern harbour walls, the Upper Barrakka Gardens are one of the city's best viewpoints and certainly worth making the climb. These shaded gardens were created in 1661 and their colonnaded terraces, adorned with statues and fountains, are a joy to navigate.

It is said that all roads lead to the sea in Valletta, making getting lost almost impossible. Due to its small size and pedestrianised centre, exploring on foot is recommended. If you wish to travel further afield, the bus network is extensive and not expensive. St Elmo Bay on the south side of Valletta is the nearest beach to the centre and an ideal swimming spot. Golden sandy shores and turquoise waters make it a popular destination for diving and snorkelling, particularly as the remains of the British vessel HMS Maori (sunk by German bombers in 1942) lie beneath the surface, its rusting wreck occupied by octopuses, cuttlefish and mullets.

Along the harbourside of Sliema there are numerous boats that offer trips and cruises around the island. Gozo and its glorious beaches are also accessible by ferry from the Grand Harbour, or you might like to take a sunset trip along the shoreline and watch the city come alight.

Useful sites
vallettaferryservices.com
visitmalta.com/en
vallettawaterfront.com

Essential information

Visit the Barrakka gardens at noon and 4pm for the firing of the cannons on the Saluting Battery.

Best time to visit Spring and autumn are perfect for exploring the city when it's cooler

Currency € Euro

Time zone UTC+1

The city was deliberately built like a fort by the Knights of Malta (of the Order of St John), the location chosen for its highly defensible position

EAST & CENTRAL

70 Krakow
72 Warsaw
73 Torun
74 Prague
75 Bucharest
74 Brasov
76 Sibiu
77 Bratislava
78 Budapest
79 Sarajevo
80 Belgrade
81 Pristina
82 Kotor
83 Ljubjana
84 Koper
85 Skopje
86 Zagreb
87 Dubrovnik
88 Sofia
89 Istanbul
90 Tiblisi

The central point of Old Kraków's Market Square is impossibly picturesque

KRAKÓW

A TOWN OF HISTORY, ARCHITECTURE AND CULTURE, POLAND'S FORMER CAPITAL HAS IT ALL

Essential information

It's considered rude to wear a hat indoors, whether that is a church, a restaurant or someone's home – so take it off if you want a warm welcome.

Best time to visit May to July

Currency zł • Polish złoty

Time zone UTC+1

Every major city has a spot that defines it; a recognisable landmark, street or situation that becomes iconic and instantly familiar. New York has Times Square, London has Tower Bridge, Tokyo has the Shibuya Crossing. While Kraków has just as many grand sights and tourist must-sees as any other city in the world, it won't take long until you find that one spot here. Old Kraków is tiny compared to the modern sprawl of the former capital, but there's a reason it was entered as one of the earliest UNESCO World Heritage Sites back in 1978. It really is the heart of the city, encircled by Planty Park and dotted with quaint restaurants, ornate buildings and 24-hour opportunities to drink vodka should you need them.

The Old Town is where much of the action is at, with the main market square – the largest in Europe – acting as the epicentre for the buzz of the city, which vibrates out onto the narrow cobbled streets. This is where Kraków's most familiar sight stands – St Mary's Basilica, the famed church whose asymmetrical spires are likely identifiable by most travel lovers. There's a mix of historic landmarks to glimpse in this market area, including the Baroque-style Kraków Cloth Hall that takes centre stage, the 1,000-year-old Church of St Adalbert, or the 13th-century Town Hall Tower. The surrounding townhouses add to the beauty of the open space, making just a stroll around the area or a quick snack at one of the many outdoor restaurants all the more captivating. Turn up at the right time and you may find the square being used for one of Kraków's many festivals and cultural events. You'll even find something to enjoy underneath the square, with the Rynek Underground museum sprawling beneath the main square and providing a look at the life of

EAST AND CENTRAL

> "The locals are more than ready to join you for a drink or three"

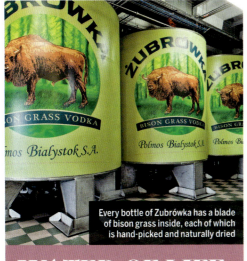

Every bottle of Zubrówka has a blade of bison grass inside, each of which is hand-picked and naturally dried

WATER OF LIFE

While it might seem like something of a cliché to say, if you're visiting Kraków then you really ought to try the country's national drink – vodka. Coming from the Polish word for water (*woda*), it isn't hard to find a place that sells vodka. Every restaurant, bar, cafe and the many 24-hour alcohol stores stock their shelves with numerous and varied bottles of the spirit.

But that doesn't mean that you should just step into any old place and order any old stuff. Like any national drink, there are degrees of quality that ultimately affect how pleasant an experience you'll have. There are vodka tasting tours, but if you'd rather avoid the tourist traps then Old Kraków is home to a number of reputable places. Ask around – the Polish are extremely friendly, despite their sourpuss demeanours, and are more than willing to offer suggestions. Failing that, look for brands like Zubrówka, Wyborowa and Chopin that will guarantee a fair example of good Polish vodka, as well as the flavoured Wisniówka. For the morning after, there's also the herbal Żołądkowa to ease the stomach.

Krakówians centuries ago. On top of a number of reconstructions of medieval structures, this novel museum uses fog and holograms to create a realistic depiction of how Kraków would have appeared 700 years ago.

With the central square finished and after a casual stroll around the myriad boutiques and eateries of the cobbled streets of Old Kraków (perhaps it's time for some Polish pierogies?), there's still one more part of the historic quarter to discover. Wandering south will bring you to the broad Vistula river, a popular destination in the summer months, where Kraków's sizeable student population makes the most of the green and well-maintained banks of the river or takes part in various water sport activities. Here, standing proud on the opposite side of the river, you'll spot Wawel Castle, a historic 14th-century fortress that has been added to over the years, spanning medieval, Renaissance and Baroque styles as a result.

A short walk down from the castle further south will take you to Kazimierz, the old Jewish District that manages to blend 16th-century synagogues and public squares with trendy restaurants, indie art galleries and cocktail bars. It's a seamless mix of modern cool with the historic, making it a great destination to end the day before heading back into the centre of the Old Town to sample Kraków's exciting nightlife. With huge clubs dotted around the central plaza and plenty more vodka bars throughout the area, Kraków can cater to any taste when it comes to parties, and the locals – a mix of Polish and international students – are more than ready to join you for a drink or three.

There's still plenty more to see besides central Kraków, however, which is also the best location from which to visit the sombre yet crucial Auschwitz. Though it will take an hour or so to reach the infamous concentration camp, there are plenty of public transport routes that will take you there, though a tour guide in the city itself can make the arrangements for you. Understandably, visiting Auschwitz is not a pleasant experience, but seeing the camp grounds and learning about its horrific history are arguably important.

You may want to enjoy a slice of history a little more uplifting, in which case a trip to the Wieliczka Salt Mines is a surprisingly fulfilling experience. The 13th-century complex was producing salt up until 2007, but will now take you 300 metres (984 feet) underground through a cavernous maze of tunnels, an underground lake and numerous statues carved into the salt rock by the miners that worked the mines. There are even four separate, ornate chapels carved into the rock, replete with reception areas and chandeliers ready to host special events and weddings. That's perhaps what's most surprising about Kraków: while it may have a number of recognisable landmarks – ones that are arguably worth the visit – it's able to provide culture, thrills and surprises in equal measure.

Useful sites
www.visitkrakow.com
www.krakowcard.com
www.auschwitz.org/en/

Take in the sights of Kraków from the comfort of a horse-drawn carriage

Auschwitz is a sombre and melancholy reminder of Europe's greatest travesty, and an essential destination if visiting Kraków

The 15th-century Corpus Christi Basilica in Kazimierz is a fine example of Gothic architecture

Warsaw's Old Town was faithfully reconstructed after World War II and is now a UNESCO World Heritage site

WARSAW

POLAND'S CAPITAL OFFERS A PERSPECTIVE ON THE COUNTRY THAT YOU WON'T GET ANYWHERE ELSE

No place is better at showing the history, food and culture that Poland has to offer than Warsaw. It provides a relaxed atmosphere that rewards the traveller who likes to wander. Today the city reflects Poland's resilience following two of the country's recent key events, World War II and reforms following the collapse of communism in Poland. The city honours its history through street art, architecture and museums, while also looking to the future with new buildings.

In 1944 the people of Warsaw began an insurrection against the German forces occupying the city – the Warsaw Uprising. In retaliation to this, the German forces began to destroy the city after the uprising ended and by the end of the war, they had destroyed over 85 percent of its buildings. Warsaw's Old Town was recreated from scratch to how it was before the war, and you can explore the Castle Square, taking in the historic sights before visiting the Royal Castle or St John's Cathedral. If you would like to see more of Poland's more recent history, the Museum of Life under Communism takes you back in time to see what post-war Poland was like. With recreations of typical apartments of the time, photos and products from that era, the museum offers a unique perspective on life in communist Poland. To get a flavour of traditional Polish food, go to one of the many milk bars around Warsaw. These are where you can find a variety of affordable dishes such as pierogi, boiled dumplings that come with either sweet or savoury fillings.

You could spend a whole day in the Praga district alone. This area was not touched during World War II and because of this there are aspects of the city that cannot be found elsewhere. There are over 100 shrines built during the war, located close to housing and courtyards and they were ways for people to worship without going too far from their homes. Each one is unique in their aesthetics. The houses are also home to contemporary street art. For fans of street art, visit the Museum of Neon, also found in the Praga district. The museum displays the largest collection of neon signs from the Cold World era.

From most parts of Warsaw you can see the Palace of Culture and Science. Constructed in 1955, it is a stunning building, having been inspired by the art deco high-rise buildings in the United States. Originally dedicated to Stalin, it stands at 237 metres (778 feet) tall and at one time had the world's tallest clock tower. Today it is home to a cinema, two museums, various pubs, an auditorium and offers excellent panoramic views of the city. There is something to do all-year round as in the summer there are various performances and shows, while in the winter there is an ice rink.

Useful sites
warsawtour.pl
poland.travel/en
pkin.pl

Essential information

For those wanting to shop, visit the Złote Tarasy. The complex has around 200 stores, 40 restaurants and even a cinema.

Best time to visit May to August

Currency zł · Polish złoty

Time zone UTC+1

EAST AND CENTRAL

The old town is crammed with medieval structures, it really feels like travelling back in time

TORUŃ

THE RED BRICK CITY OF POLAND THAT CELEBRATES THE STARS…

With around 200,000 people living in Toruń, it's certainly on the smaller side of the cities contained within this book. Of course this makes it perfect for a quick weekend break, or as a part of an itinerary for a bigger trip across Poland. Whatever your particular situation, don't let the smaller stature of this historic city trick you into thinking it doesn't have what it takes to lull you away from the big names in Poland tourism, like Warsaw, Kraków or Gdańsk. For one thing, it's very much a place that manages to pick a vibe and stick with it: Gothic architecture fills the city, both from the major tourist landmarks to the everyday property. It *feels* medieval to walk around its cobbled streets, to gaze on its brick exteriors or look down on its red-tiled roofs. It's really a very pretty place to behold, and Toruń bewilders any who visit thanks to its ye olde charm. This is likely a contributing factor to the fact that the city itself is a registered UNESCO heritage site.

Those landmarks aren't going to be far to trek to from the main old town square, which is itself a must-visit destination. Taking a glimpse down on the city from the old town hall tower (which you'll spot thanks to its iconic black and gold clock) will help you to draw in the consistent look of Toruń. It'll cost you 21 zloty (about $5) to clamber to the top, but time your trip well and you can do it for free on Wednesdays. From there you'll want to tick off St John's church, the Leaning Tower of Toruń and the numerous statues and monuments that are scattered about the old town. Most noteworthy here is the monument dedicated to Nicolaus Copernicus, the famous astronomer who shook the world's understanding of our galaxy and whose home is also available to visit.

Aside from all of this, you'll do well to spare some time for a quiet stroll along the promenade of the Vistula River. It runs alongside the old medieval walls to really accentuate the beauty of the city, but in the summer months it's a popular spot for locals and tourists alike as they descend on the stepped banks of the river. It's worth a little hike over the bridge and the river to the other side, however, especially if you time it for sunset and ultimately nightfall. It's at this point that the lights come up and the whole city reveals its gorgeous sparkling evening wear. There isn't much to see on the opposite bank of the river, but a chance to glimpse this quaint medieval town looking its best is definitely going to be worth the walk.

Useful sites
visittorun.pl
kopernik.com.pl
poland.travel/en/cities/torun-the-city-of-many-nations

Essential information

A lot of the old town in Toruń is pedestrianised. Something to be aware of if your visit to Poland includes a car.

Best time to visit Late summer for good weather but fewer tourists

Currency zł · Polish złoty

Time zone UTC+1

Copernicus is understandably an important part of Toruń's history, so you'll see references throughout the city

PRAGUE

EXPLORE THE STUNNING ATTRACTIONS OF THE CZECH REPUBLIC'S CAPITAL CITY

Prague is nicknamed the 'city of a hundred spires', but it doesn't take long before you realise this architectural gem, nestled within the Czech Republic and cut through by the Vltava River, cannot solely be defined by such a single set of features. Naot withstanding the fact that it's factually incorrect – there are more than 1,000 spires, turrets, steeples and towers gently punching the air over this capital city – Prague can be anything to anyone: romantic, fashionable, artistic, bustling and quiet on the one hand; a foodie's paradise, eclectic watering hole or simply a chocolate-box feast for the eyes on the other.

Take a boat ride soon after you arrive and you can soak up the splendour of those medieval buildings, unspoiled by war and modern development, before putting your feet on firm ground in pursuit of the key attractions. Get your timing right and you'll be able to see the world's oldest working astronomical clock in action, a thing of beauty that dates back to 1410 and stands in the Old Town Square. A performance takes place every hour where four animated figures shake their heads to the ring of a bell while the 12 apostles filter past two open windows to the amazement of the massed crowds.

From there, you can make your way over to the Jewish Quarter, a historical area in which Jews were once restricted to living. There are six glorious synagogues, an old cemetery, the 18th-century Old Jewish Town Hall, and many monuments and artefacts that form the Jewish Museum in Prague. They can be seen by purchasing an entry ticket, and it's worth paying for the Old New Synagogue alone – it's Europe's oldest surviving and active synagogue, and steeped in legend.

Prague's compact nature means you can easily get around on foot. South of the Jewish Quarter is Charles Bridge, crossing the Vltava and enabling crowds to mass along a walkway some ten-metres (33-feet) wide. Construction of the bridge began in 1357, and it has seen numerous battles and natural disasters since then. Most notable here are 30 mostly Baroque statues and statuaries positioned across its length of 621 metres (2,037 feet). They're all replicas today, with the originals removed for safe keeping, but they're no less striking for it.

It certainly hasn't affected Prague's status as one of UNESCO's World Heritage Sites, and that's little wonder. Each twist and turn of Prague's narrow streets offers up copious delights, and while you'll be charged to visit many of the splendid attractions, there's plenty to do for free. Wandering the complex around Prague Castle, which contains the Bohemian Crown Jewels, will cost nothing (although entry will). There's also a huge, bronze horse statue (a monument to Hussite General Jan Žižka on Vitkov Hill, and free tours of the Rudolfinum concert hall.

Whatever you do, though, don't leave without visiting the New Town, in particular the politically iconic Wenceslas Square and the National Museum. Be sure to also sample the traditional Czech soup kulajda; the thin pancakes called palacinky; or vepro-knedlo-zelo, which is roast pork, bread dumplings and stewed cabbage. Such food goes down well with beer, which is just as well since it is plentiful and cheap, and there are many breweries that encourage visitors. Just take it easy: with so much to see and do, you'll want a clear head come the morning, although a stroll around Letná Park may help – as long as you don't stop for a drink in its beer garden.

Essential information

Watch out for currency scams offering 0% commission – and don't exchange on the streets of Prague!

Best time to visit Spring and early autumn (for milder weather)
Currency Kč • Czech Koruna
Time zone UTC+1

Useful sites
www.prague.eu/en
www.hrad.cz/en
www.jewishmuseum.cz/en/info/visit

Of Prague's 18 bridges, Charles bridge is its most famous, for its rich history and 'love locks'

Church of Our Lady before Týn by the Old Town Square

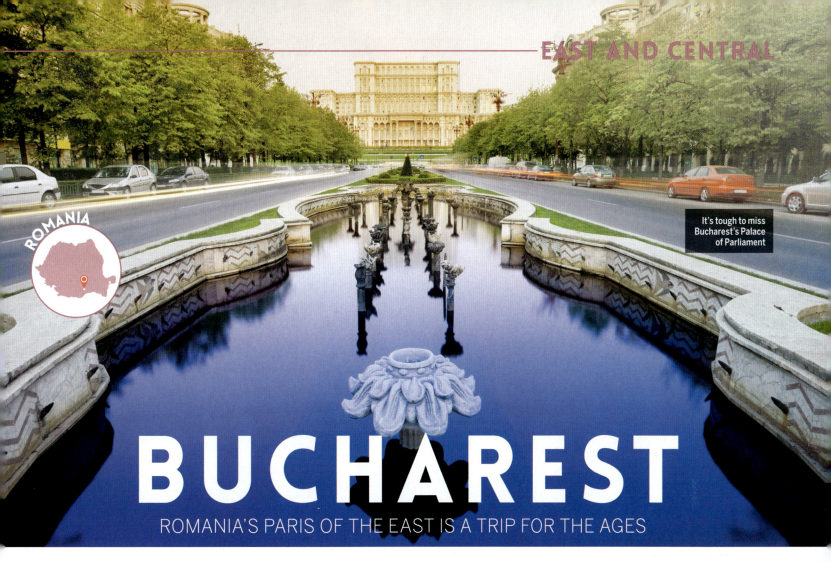

It's tough to miss Bucharest's Palace of Parliament

EAST AND CENTRAL

BUCHAREST

ROMANIA'S PARIS OF THE EAST IS A TRIP FOR THE AGES

Romania's unique position in Europe – both geographical and historical – means that it offers an experience like no other on the continent. Situated in southeast Europe, it borders a former Yugoslavian country, a couple of former Soviet Union countries and the Black Sea, which makes for a fascinating hotpot of wildly different cultures. Nowhere is this smorgasbord of influence more keenly displayed than in its capital, Bucharest.

Not for nothing is Bucharest called the Paris of the East. The city is awash with stunning architecture, striking religious buildings, high-end retail and mouthwatering food.

Starting with the architecture, the Palace of Parliament is a must-visit. Started in 1984 under President Nicolae Ceausescu, it is the largest administrative building, the heaviest and also the most expensive administrative building in the world, containing around one million tonnes of Romanian marble. Tours need to be pre-booked and it's worth doing. Ceausescu's influence can be seen all over the city, having rebuilt the city following an earthquake in 1977. Grandiose opulence was his watchword, as is the case with many dictators.

To take a further step back in time, enjoy a stroll down Calea Victoriei. This street houses many of Bucharest's most beautiful and iconic buildings, many of which have stood since the 19th century. Highlights include Cantacuzino Palace (now a music museum), the Yellow House, Revolution Square and the Telephone Palace. Little wonder this street is known as the Champs-Elysee of Bucharest. The city is a fascinating clash of gorgeous old buildings, vast Communist-era vanity projects and modern neighbourhoods, offering a little something for all tastes.

Faith is a huge part of Romanian life and you won't go far before stumbling across a jaw-dropping religious building. The St Nicholas Russian Church is a sight not to be missed with its multiple domed spires, the Stavropoleos Monastery is the opposite, an understated yet elegant building, while the Roman Patriarchal Cathedral holds the bones of Dimitri Basarabov, Patron Saint of Bucharest.

Other sights to enjoy around Bucharest include the Dimitrie Gusti National Village Museum. This outdoor museum is filled with traditional houses and villages, showing visitors how Romanians from all over the country used to live. If you like your history, Old Town is worth a visit to see Manuc's Inn, which is one of Romania's oldest buildings. If you need to recuperate after all that sightseeing, the Therme Bucharest is Europe's largest geothermal bath complex.

Romanian food follows the same pattern. The flavours and portions in Romanian cooking are big to say the least. The cuisine is heavily meat-based, with pork a particular favourite. Chiftele (meatballs with shredded potato and carrot), sarmale (minced pork and rice wrapped in cabbage leaves), tochitura moldoveneasca (pork stew topped with a fried egg) and ciorba (beef tripe soup) are all among the popular dishes that you have to try to experience authentic Bucharest. For the sweet-toothed traveller, papanasi (cottage cheese-filled doughnuts topped with jam and cream) are also worth a try.

The food, the architecture – both historical and communist – and the religious fervour all seem to take a bit of inspiration from Romania's very different neighbours. This means Bucharest should certainly be high up on your list if you want to experience a little bit of everything in one bustling, cosmopolitan city.

Useful sites
visitbucharest.today
romaniatourism.com/bucharest.html
www.introducingbucharest.com

Essential information

If you visit the Old Town then sturdy shoes are a must as the cobblestones can be very unforgiving for anyone wearing heels or sandals.

Best time to visit Spring is the best season to visit Bucharest, both for the weather and green spaces

Currency lei • Romanian leu

Time zone UTC+2

Brașov Council Square: in the Brothers Grimm version of The Pied Piper of Hamelin, the children dig their way to Translyvania and surface here

BRAȘOV

IN THE RUGGED HEART OF TRANSYLVANIA LIES AN UNDERRATED JEWEL

The medieval look and feel of Brașov transport you instantly back in time. Immerse yourself in the history by walking the Old Town's fortifications, making sure to wander pass the 464-year-old Catherine's Gate, the only original city gate to survive from the medieval period. Keeping with the theme, visit the Biserica Neagră, the largest Gothic church in eastern Europe, for £2 ($3). In the evening, a guided tour by candlelight is available for £23 ($28), taking you through the city streets to the sounds of history and legend – not to mention a ghost or two, and a vampire tale for good measure.

Speaking of vampires, a trip to Transylvania wouldn't be complete without visiting Bran Castle, reportedly the inspiration for the home of Dracula. Whether this is true or not, the castle is certainly worth visiting – 30 kilometres (19 miles) from Brașov, the half-hourly bus from the city takes 45 minutes and costs £1 ($2) each way. There are a lot of tourist shops and cafes, however, so if you think that this might spoil the history, mystique, and legend for you, opt instead for Peleș Castle, one of the most beautiful in Europe. It's worth taking the train for a breathtaking journey through the richly forested Bucegi Mountains.

Back in Brașov, an infamous sight is the Hollywood-style "Brașov" sign erected in the hills. Reach it via the Mt Tampa cable car for £3 ($4) return, although queues can be extreme in the summer and the operating hours seem to vary on a whim. Alternatively, a hike to the top only requires an hour of your time and some shoes with good grip – just make sure to stay on the path and away from wild boars (and possibly bears).

Foodies have plenty of reason to rejoice – the absolutely delectable treat of papanași awaits, traditional fried doughnuts made with soft cheese, slathered with jam, and topped off with a doughnut ball. If you're travelling over Christmas, don't miss the beautiful Council Square Christmas market and its vin fiert. Any time of year, La Ceaun welcomes you with its famous ciorba de fasole (bean soup), alongside the "cooked in a cauldron" delights and traditional Romanian bulz.

As Brașov is the second-largest city in Transylvania, it's easily accessible from Bucharest by train in 2.5 hours for £10 ($12), although the trains are notoriously slow. If you hire a car, make sure to make time for a day trip to the Transfăgărășan Highway – the stark beauty of the winding mountain road speaks for itself. To venture further into Romania's wild nature, visit the Seven Ladders Canyon, 12 kilometres (7 miles) from Brasov and a reasonable £2 ($2) to navigate boardwalks and bridges, through crevices and past waterfalls. Pay £17 ($21) more and you can zipline your way back down.

Finish back in Brașov with a shot of traditional tuica (plum brandy) or a glass of summer socata (elderflower juice) and your city trip is complete.

Essential information

Babele and the Sphinx are busy tourist traps; valuable travel time is better spent elsewhere.

Best time to visit Late spring or early autumn (to avoid peak tourist season)

Currency lei · Romanian leu

Time zone UTC+2

Useful sites
cfrcalatori.ro
brasovcity.ro
romaniatourism.com/index.html

Bună!

EAST AND CENTRAL

SIBIU

WHATEVER YOU DO IN THIS ROMANIAN CITY, DON'T TELL A LIE...

There are a lot of cities like Sibiu in Eastern Europe, comparatively small places largely forgotten in the world of tourism thanks to their nearby neighbours hogging all the limelight. But it's for the best, because taking some time out to visit these sorts of places is often more rewarding than the 'obvious' destinations. In the case of Sibiu, it's got a peculiar history that does seem to have shaped a lot of what is there for visitors to get the most out of.

It was a German settlement, originally, and that has influenced a lot of its heritage, but what is especially curious is how it truly is a city of two halves. Historically the upper town was for the wealthy, the pious and the well-to-do, while the lower town was for the poor labourers. To look at it, you'd likely assume the same is true today, since the upper town – which is where many of the city's landmarks and notable spots are to be found – has received the brunt of the maintenance money. However, each half is worth exploring, and in truth you won't truly have visited Sibiu without a stroll around the lower town. Here the streets are narrower and more winding, leading to tiny squares, local markets and cute little cafes and restaurants. It's well noted for its small colourful buildings, which still manage to inspire awe even with their varying degrees of degradation.

The upper town, conversely, is a little more refined. The two main squares here are the Piața Mare and Piața Mică (literally Grand Square and Little Square), and between the two you'll find most of the major sights. At the Little Square, look for an iron wrought bridge over a winding path below; this is the first iron bridge in Romania, but crucially is known as the Bridge of Lies. There are a number of myths regarding the powers of this bridge, with the grandest of them all suggesting that a big enough lie – when told on the bridge – will cause it to collapse. At the huge expanse that is the Grand Square, you'll find the majority of the churches, museums and the city hall of Sibiu. You'll also have plenty of choice when it comes to restaurants and cafes, though you might feel you're being watched as you sip your coffee: that's just the iconic Sibiu "eyes"; little ventilating windows in the roofs of some buildings that give the impression of the building having numerous eyes.

But perhaps more interesting than all of that is the connections between the two halves of the city. Well-known for its winding streets, these connecting stairways add a good sprinkle of quaintness about your city exploration. Most popular of these is the aptly named Stairs Passage, which actually has a cobbled slope careening its way between the two parts of the city. All of this makes Sibiu a city that is incredibly rewarding for those who love to wander about, yet doesn't really ask very much of those who visit.

Useful sites
romaniatourism.com/sibiu.html
sibiu-turism.ro/About-us.aspx
whc.unesco.org/en/tentativelists/1929/

Essential information

The nearby ASTRA open-air museum is one of the largest of its kind, with 98 hectares and over 400 buildings – well worth making time for.

Best time to visit May to September
Currency lei · Romanian leu
Time zone UTC+2

A lot of rumour and myth surrounds the Bridge of Lies, so better to be honest around it

BRATISLAVA

DISCOVER A CITY THAT LOOKS AT THE WORLD FROM A DIFFERENT ANGLE

For centuries, Slovakia was under the rule of larger, more dominant states. It was part of the Austria-Hungarian Empire until the end of World War I, when the Slovaks and Czechs formed Czechoslovakia. The country was occupied by Nazi Germany during World War II, before the Soviet Union called the shots for around four decades. However, in 1993 Czechoslovakia peacefully broke up, forming the two separate countries of Czech Republic and Slovakia. Now it's their chance to shine. Over the past 30 years Slovakia has been developing its position as an independent sovereign nation while still retaining the influences of their past.

Bratislava was chosen as the new country's capital due to its important position on the Danube river as well as the borders with Austria and Hungary. It is rapidly gaining a reputation as a popular tourist destination with its stunning historical landmarks, affordability and some iconic quirky attractions.

An essential stop on any trip to Bratislava has to be Bratislava Castle. Standing high on a hill above the Danube, the castle has existed in one form or another for well over 1,000 years, guarding the city and country from invaders. The current iteration is an imposing 17th-century Baroque-style building that offers amazing views of the city, as well as Austria and Hungary. The castle houses the Slovak Museum of History, which includes a goldsmith and silversmith that is well worth a visit.

Beyond the castle, Bratislava's Old Town is where you'll find many of the city's gems. Michael's Gate is a beautiful route into the area, a striking white, copper-roofed tower that you can ascend for a small fee to enjoy unrivalled views. A short stroll around its paved and cobbled streets will reward you with some gorgeous old buildings such as Primate's Palace and Old Town Hall, while the town square is a charming place to relax with a coffee.

It's not all steps back in time, however. Bratislava is a rapidly modernising city, so those who want a slightly faster-paced city break can enjoy the Eurovea waterfront or the UFO observation deck above Most SNP bridge.

Bratislava isn't without its surprises and one of its most popular sights is Čumil, otherwise known as The Watcher or Man at Work. This is a statue of a workman peeking cheekily out of a manhole, checking out the feet walking by or, more commonly, stopping for a photo. Čumil is one of a number of unique statues scattered around Bratislava, which include a Napoleonic soldier and a former resident of Bratislava known for tipping his hat to all he met. Another rarity is The Church of St Elizabeth, known as The Blue Church. It's away from the main attractions, but it's definitely something many people enjoy making the time for.

Food in Bratislava has a strong Hungarian vibe, with goulash, sauerkraut and sausage soup, and a dish called bryndzové halušky (dumplings, cheese and bacon) all featuring prominently. Food is hearty, plentiful and usually reasonably priced, while the same can also be said for the beer.

Bratislava really is a hidden central-European gem of a city that has a lot going for it as a tourist destination culturally, socially and economically. Just keep an eye out for any lurking workman who decides to make an unexpected appearance!

Useful sites

visitbratislava.com
slovakia.com/cities/bratislava
welcometobratislava.eu/why-visit-bratislava

Essential information

The Bratislava Card is a great money-saving purchase if you plan on using public transport and entering museums and other attractions.

Best time to visit The Bratislava Botanical Gardens are open from April to October

Currency € · Euro

Time zone UTC+1

Bratislava Castle is an attraction to be enjoyed from afar and up close

EAST AND CENTRAL

Budapest comes alive at night, with its infamous ruin bars among the coolest places in the world to be

BUDAPEST

THE PEARL OF THE DANUBE HAS PLENTY OF SECRETS TO UNCOVER

Since it is divided into two halves of Buda and Pest, the side of the Danube you choose to stay on in Hungary's capital perhaps says as much about you as it does the city itself. The former, on the west bank, is typified by its grand panoramic views over the city below, with a rather relaxed atmosphere as you stroll about the Castle District – though you may fancy taking the 19th century funicular to the top rather than brave the many steps to reach Fisherman's Bastion. Pest, on the other hand, is the busier downtown area, meaning it's here you'll want to go for exciting spots to eat, drink and party in equal measure.

As a tourist destination, Budapest is crammed with things to do. Architecturally, it's one of the most fascinating in all of Europe, ranging from its ornate, stuccoed buildings that line any street to the grandiose structures like the Parliament or St Stephen's Basilica. Taking in all this grandeur is best done on the historic tram line two, which for the cost of just one ticket (roughly 90p/$1.15) will let you take in the impressive sights of Széchenyi Bridge, Buda Castle, Gresham Palace, Gellért Hill and so much more besides. The ride is only made all the better when disembarking at the copper-green Liberty Bridge, where the nearby Great Market Hall has everything from traditional goulash soup to the popular street food snack lángos – deep-fried discs of dough served with cheese and sour cream.

You won't be lacking for choices when the Sun goes down, either. From Michelin-star restaurants like Onyx to gourmet burgers and fries at Zing Burger, Budapest is capable of catering for all tastes. This is particularly true of its party scene, too, which is primarily situated within the old Jewish Quarter. Gozsdu Courtyard is the centre of Budapest's nightlife, and you'll find the famous ruin bars only a short distance from here. A taste of the national drink pálinka is made all the more enjoyable (or tolerable) within Szimpla Kert, the complex of funkily decorated buildings that kickstarted the city's unique ruin bar scene. You'll be thankful for Budapest's numerous thermal baths the morning after, then, with the baroque-style Széchenyi Baths that sit in the middle of City Park being the most popular place to wash away the late-night grogginess.

In addition to the countless historical and cultural museums, a plethora of unique tours – try a city drive in a classic Trabant – and large, central parks, it might surprise you just how much there is to do in Budapest.

Useful sites
www.budapest.com
welovebudapest.com/en
www.bathsbudapest.com

Essential information

🇭🇺 The 100E bus from the airport will get you into downtown Pest within 40 minutes, but as an express service it's slightly pricier.

Best time to visit Spring and autumn (to avoid the high heat and freezing cold)

Currency Ft • Hungarian Forint

Time zone UTC+1

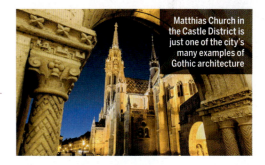

Matthias Church in the Castle District is just one of the city's many examples of Gothic architecture

There are numerous ornate buildings to ogle as you wander the city, but the Parliament remains the crown jewel

Szia!

SARAJEVO

AT THE FOOT OF A BALKAN MOUNTAIN LIES A BRIDGE BETWEEN TWO CULTURES

Dubbed the city where east meets west, Sarajevo's mountain setting and Ottoman bazaars make it a cultural hotpot for visitors who long for a diverse travelling experience. The capital of Bosnia and Herzegovina, tourism in the city is on the rise after word of its magic got around – and fast.

Sarajevo is tucked away in a long, narrow valley with woodland and mountains on either side, giving visitors a glimpse of its stunning backdrop. Thankfully, the surrounding mountains are easily accessible due to Sarajevo's expansive cable car system, making it the perfect introduction to the city. A return ticket costs around £10, or 20 Convertible Marks, and it takes approximately nine minutes to get from the bottom to the very top. The breathtaking views from the summit will make it impossible to leave, particularly when sunset falls and drenches the city in twilight.

The city is decorated with beautiful mosques and Catholic churches, but the main pedestrian walkway, Ferhadija, is where the city really takes on a distinctive character of its own. Visitors are often seen taking photos from the middle of the street, looking down towards either end. This is the point where western shop signs, pubs and bars meet the Turkish bazaar. At one end of the street, traditional coffee houses and hookah pipes reign supreme and no alcohol is to be served, and at the other, men and women can be seen lining bars with a pint of beer or glass of wine in their hands. If you have a sweet tooth, you can pick up a delicious ice cream for as little as £1 by an array of vendors.

If the city's Ottoman architecture makes you want to know more about this fascinating period of Bosnian history, you must go to Seher-Cehaja bridge, over the Miljacka river. It's a sight to behold. The stunning piece of construction can be translated as the 'Mayor's Bridge' from the original Turkish. The 15th-century bridge is one of 13 in Sarajevo. Its initial design consisted of five arches, but it's since been renovated and changed dozens of times, and one of the arches has been walled up and covered with a road.

The city is also scattered with thought-provoking museums that shed light on the tragedy of recent war in Bosnia, and the two decades of healing it has taken to make its capital a tourist hotspot.

To end your day in the most relaxing way possible, pay a visit to the hamam, which can be found along the river. Opt for a massage or aromatherapy treatment, and let the therapists take you back to the city's Ottoman glory days, making you feel like a sultan (or sultana) living the high life in Bosnia's mountainous capital.

Useful sites
visitsarajevo.ba/?lang=en
sarajevo.travel
sarajevofunkytours.com

Essential information

Sarajevo can be very traditional in places, so be careful to respect any local conventions you encounter.

Best time to visit May to October

Currency KM · Bosnia-Herzegovina Convertible Mark

Time zone UTC+1

"The breathtaking views from the summit will make it impossible to leave"

Zadravo!

EAST AND CENTRAL

BELGRADE

THE BALKAN CAPITAL THAT OFFERS IT ALL

If variety is the spice of life, then Belgrade is one spicy city. There are a lot of aspects to a visit to the Serbian capital, and its mix of experiences is unmatched among the other Balkan counterparts. Placed at the point where the Danube and the Sava rivers converge, it's been an important historical location for years. That's likely why the Kalemegdan fortress at Belgrade's centre, which once housed an entire city, was such an important part of the capital's identity. These days it's a rather impressive public space functioning as a park, an open air museum, restaurant and cafe and even a zoo. It's a big part of any trip to Belgrade, so it's worth starting there – in fact, it's highly likely you'll end up there more than once. It really is that significant.

Stretching out from the fortress is the Knez Mihailova shopping street, a long and significant pedestrian route that will take you past a number of the more important museums, the national art gallery and Republic Square and ultimately further on down to the church of Saint Sava. The street itself is home to numerous bars, restaurants and cafes, and is a common meeting point for locals – making it a great place for people watching. A lot of Belgrade branches off from this important route, so it's good to get familiar with it.

But Belgrade is a city that is capable of providing a very rich visit, and that's particularly true of its nightlife. While there is obviously a lot to visit in the central downtown area, Belgrade has a culture of partying on boats, known as splav, which you can find moored to the southwest of the main city centre and they come in a variety of shapes and sizes to suit all tastes. Nearby is also the popular Ada Ciganlija, a huge natural parkland jutting out into the Sava river. It's particularly noteworthy on hotter days thanks to its beach and the seaside-resort vibes – replete with water sports and sundrenched parties – that can make you feel completely removed from the city life.

Belgrade adds to its variety in the form of two particular neighbourhoods: Skadarlija and Zemun. The former is a bohemian 'quarter', built of cobblestones and cute storefronts, offering a distinct and laid-back vibe thanks to its quaint appearance, outstanding traditional restaurants and its artist-infused lifestyle. Zemun, on the other hand, is only now *technically* a part of Belgrade – prior to the 1934 was actually its own town. Though it is a little ways out from the city proper, it's very visibly its own place with different architecture, different accents and a different way of life. It's something completely unlike downtown Belgrade, and worth visiting for its seafood restaurants and the view from the top of Gardoš hill.

Useful sites
tob.rs/en
belgradeatnight.com/festivals-in-belgrade
serbia.travel/en

Essential information

The topic of Kosovo is still not one to broach lightly. Better to avoid the topic altogether and certainly be wary if you plan to travel further south.

Best time to visit Late spring or early autumn to avoid the high heats of summer

Currency din · Serbian Dinar

Time zone UTC+1

European cities are rife with castles and fortresses, but few are as central to the city's culture as in Belgrade

Zdravo!

PRISTINA

KOSOVO'S MOUNTAINS AND MEDIEVAL ARCHITECTURE HAS SEEN IT RISE FROM THE ASHES

Essential information

Do as the locals do and enjoy a nightly xhiro – a ritual evening walk through a town's main streets.

Best time to visit Spring, when the country is green and less busy

Currency € · Turkish Lira

Time zone UTC+1

How to get there Flights can be taken into Pristina International Airport from many of Europe's main hubs, or you could catch a bus or train from neighbouring countries

As far as hidden gems go, Kosovo is one of the most elusive. It's a country many find difficult to find on a map; a territory that declared independence from Serbia in 2008, it is still unrecognised by just under half of the United Nations member states.

Scarred by the armed conflict that saw it battling against the Federal Republic of Yugoslavia between February 1998 and June 1999, Kosovo has found it difficult to shake off associations with the war. Yet you ignore Kosovo at your peril. For this is a safe and hospitable country that, while still remaining off the typical tourist trail, will always welcome visitors. There are the delightful Ottoman influences in its capital Pristina, for starters, where it's hard not to marvel at its four historically protected mosques, the 15th-century baths and the Kosovo museum built in 1889.

The city changed hugely following a decision by the ruling communists in 1947 to "destroy the old, build the new" (check out the unusually styled National Library). But go for the culture, the nightlife and the restaurants serving a mix of traditional dishes and international cuisine and you'll never leave disappointed.

Venture further out and you can enjoy the picturesque mountain towns nestled amid lush countryside. Make time for Prizren's old town, one of Kosovo's oldest rural settlements, dating back over two thousand years. Here you'll find the former base of the Albanian Defence League (a group of nationalists who fought for freedom from the Ottomans). Prizren's religious landmarks include its 15th-century Bajrakli Mosque, as well as the 14th-century Serbian Orthodox church, Our Lady of Ljeviš, built amid beautiful medieval cobbled streets.

For those who love the great outdoors, be sure to visit the hiking haven of the Rugova Valley, which offers plenty of activities for the adventurous, including skiing and zip-lining. Greater tranquillity can be found at the wine-growing village of Velika Hoca where there are 13 Orthodox churches to explore, many dating to the Serbian Middle Ages.

Useful sites
beinkosovo.com
viewkosova.com
kosovo-info.com

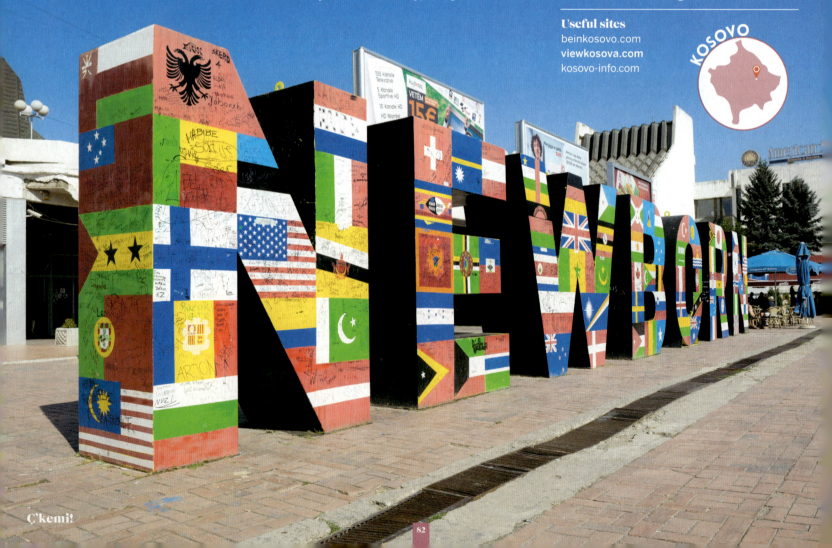

EAST AND CENTRAL

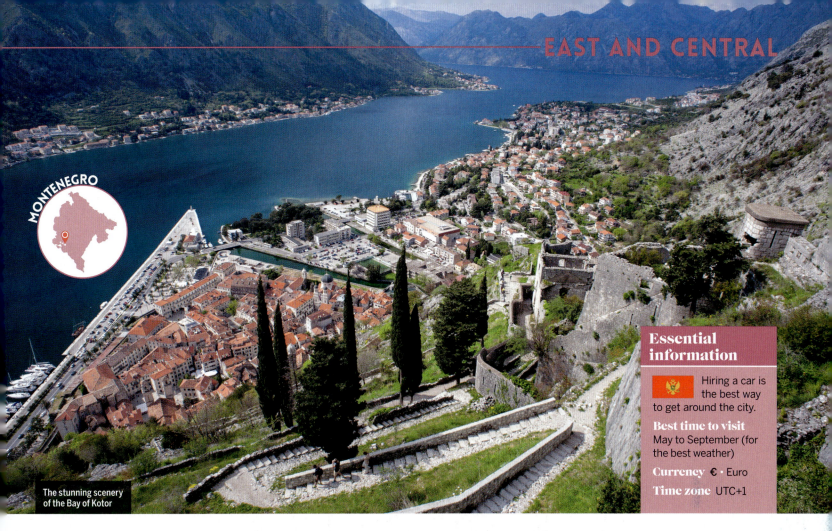

The stunning scenery of the Bay of Kotor

Essential information

Hiring a car is the best way to get around the city.

Best time to visit May to September (for the best weather)

Currency € · Euro

Time zone UTC+1

KOTOR

DISCOVER THIS PICTURESQUE AND UNDERRATED MEDIEVAL COASTAL CITY

Located on the coast of Montenegro, Kotor is one of the country's most historic cities and is over 2,000 years old. In fact, the region of Kotor – including the inner Bay of Kotor, the Old Town and the fortifications – is listed as a UNESCO World Heritage Site. The fortifications that surround Kotor date back to the 15th century, when the city was managed by the Venetian Republic.

It is hardly a surprise that Kotor, considered to be one of the best-preserved medieval cities in the Adriatic sea, is filled with breathtaking medieval architecture. As you walk down to the Old Town and wander through its cobbled streets, you will see countless medieval churches, palaces and cathedrals – such as the Cathedral of Saint Tryphon – that will leave you in awe. The Old Town is also a cultural hub filled with boutiques, bookshops, cafes and much more to explore. If you want to see as much of the Old Town as possible, join one of the walking tours to really fill your boots.

As a coastal city, it is not a surprise that Kotor has a rich nautical history. Whether you love naval history or you simply want to learn more about it, be sure to pay a visit to the Maritime Museum. If you fancy checking out a museum that offers something a little different, then Kotor also houses some unique hidden gems. For example, there is the Cats Museum, whose proceeds help to feed the city's cats, or Namfleg, which is an interactive jewellery and watch museum.

Aside from Kotor's historic roots, it is the perfect place for hikers to explore, and many choose to hike up the mountains to the Castle of San Giovanni, where you will be treated to scenic views of the city.

If you want to get off your feet after all that walking, why not go for a drive around the Kotor Serpentine, a winding cliffside road that provides stunning vistas of the city and the sea? Speaking of the sea, you could also hire a boat or jump on one of the many boat tours available to really experience the Bay of Kotor. For those of you who would rather stay on land, head down to Kotor's charming beaches to relax and unwind.

Kotor comes to life at night and it is perfect for sitting outside, sipping drinks and listening to the live music that can be found throughout its many bars and cafes. After a long day of exploring, enjoy a pint of Montenegro's most popular beer, the local favourite Nikšićko lager.

Just outside the Old Town walls lies the market known as Gradska Pijaca, where you can sample a vast range of local delicacies during the day.

While more tourists are flocking to Kotor each year, it is still a relatively hidden gem in comparison to other popular European destinations and it is well worth a visit.

Useful sites
visit-montenegro.com/destinations/kotor
kotor.travel

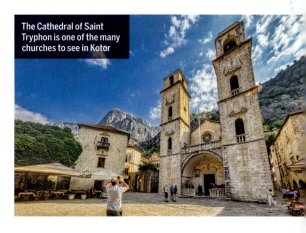

The Cathedral of Saint Tryphon is one of the many churches to see in Kotor

Zdravo!

LJUBLJANA
CAFE CULTURE AND CREATIVITY DEFINE THIS INTERESTINGLY GREEN CITY

With similar vibes to Amsterdam, the slow pace of Ljubljana makes this the perfect place for a weekend or base to explore the rest of Slovenia.

Ljubljana is the capital and largest city in Slovenia – it is also one of Europe's greenest cities. The Old Town of Ljubljana is centred around the medieval castle that sits perched on top of a hill, the streets in the centre are car-free, meaning that pedestrians are free to roam, and cafes spill out onto the city's streets and along the bank of the Ljubljanica River, which flows through the city's heart.

There are various ways to access the castle, but the easiest and perhaps most novel is the 70-metre (230-feet) funicular that leaves from the Old Town near the market on Vodnik Square. If you don't fancy heading in to the castle itself, it is free to explore the grounds; however, we'd highly recommend the 90-minute tours that are led by costumed guides.

If puppets are your thing then head to the Museum of Puppetry – it explores the world of puppetry, from the manufacture of marionettes and glove puppets to the staging of the shows – it's very interactive.

If you are feeling brave, head to Hot Horse, located in Park Tivoli, for a horse burger topped with whatever toppings take your fancy. It's just a simple takeaway joint, but horse burgers are something of a local delicacy – and the burgers are huge!

To see a different side of the city, head to Metelkova Mesto, which is an abandoned barracks that was transformed into one of the largest urban squats in Europe. Don't let that put you off, though – the graffiti and artwork that covers the buildings is incredible, and absolutely worth a look. Metelkova Mesto has a number of clubs that host concerts, club nights, and one-off music events featuring underground artists and DJs from around the world. The centre also hosts art performances, exhibitions and an occasional festival.

Taking an organised bus tour to Lake Bled for the day is a must if you are in Ljubljana for more than the weekend. With its beautifully blue waters and picturesque surroundings, Lake Bled is a travel photographer's dream – its painterly scenery has to be seen to be believed, though. And it might sound odd, but the Bled Cream Cake (kremšnita) is a culinary must for any visit to the area.

Useful sites
www.slovenia.info
www.ljubljana.si/en
www.visitljubljana.com/en/visitors

Essential information

If you miss the airport bus to the city, try one of the shared taxis – it's quicker and around the same price.

Best time to visit May to October
Currency € · Euro
Time zone UTC+1

Cafe culture is huge here, with tables lining the river bank

Živjo!

EAST AND CENTRAL

There have been a lot of eras of development for Koper, but the 15th century was its biggest moment

Essential information

Unsurprisingly considering its location, Koper is officially a bilingual city: either Italian or Slovene.

Best time to visit Between August and September to enjoy the big festivals

Currency € · Euro

Time zone UTC+1

KOPER

FOR THOSE LOOKING FOR SOMETHING DIFFERENT FROM THEIR TRIP TO SLOVENIA…

Ask the average person on the street what they most associate with Slovenia, and the chances are high that they'll pick the natural beauty of its lakes, its mountains and perhaps its capital of Ljubljana. With only 47 kilometres (29 miles) of coastline, Slovenia is unsurprisingly not well known for its beachside resorts. Koper is the oldest and largest coastal city in Slovenia, and the country's main destination for seaside tourism – while still being filled with rich history and culture. Its picturesque harbour, cobblestone streets and its stunning views of the Adriatic Sea make for a very memorable experience.

The main attraction in Koper is the city's old town, which is a must-see for anyone visiting the city. This area of the city is full of winding streets lined with stunning Venetian-style architecture and quaint cafes. Exploring the old town will reward you with the discovery of countless interesting shops, restaurants and monuments. Tito Square is the central point of the city and its most iconic spot, and since it's surrounded by many of the most important landmarks of the city, it's a great starting point. Most notably here is the Loggia Palace and the Praetorian Palace, both of which date back to the 15th century and are much loved for their well kept Gothic Venetian architecture. The stunning Praetorian Palace was even once the seat of the Venetian governor.

And let's not forget that Koper is also home to some of the most beautiful beaches in Slovenia, making it a perfect combination of sunbathing and swimming with one of the richest histories of all cities in the area. Koper dates back to 330 BCE; something to think about as you take a dip to cool off in the Adriatic sunshine. Visitors can also take part in some of the many activities the area has to offer, such as sailing, kayaking, and scuba diving. There are also plenty of boat tours available that take visitors to some of the most breathtaking islands in the Mediterranean.

The city is also home to some of the most unique and interesting festivals in Slovenia, including the Koper Summer Festival and the Koper Carnival. Be sure to keep an eye on the key events of the city when planning your holiday, and try to fit in an itinerary that suits your tastes. Whether it's popular contemporary music, gourmet food or traditional folk dancing, food or culture: Koper can probably provide a festival for you.

It's also worth thinking about Koper's geological location, which not only provides immediate access to day trips into the mainline of Slovenia but also easy excursions into Italy and Croatia for flavours of other cultures. Koper will surprise you and definitely has its own unique place within Slovenia, but as part of a bigger trip along the Adriatic, it is a must-include into your schedule.

Useful sites
visitkoper.si/en
portoroz.si/en/discover/slovenian-istria/koper/events
rail.cc/koper/ferry/c

Zdravo!

SKOPJE

THE BALKAN CITY THAT OFFERS IT ALL WILL SURPRISE EVEN THE MOST WELL-TRAVELLED OF TRAVELLERS...

There's a moment that everyone new to Skopje will experience, a moment that leaves an indelible mark on the wanderer's mind. Back in 2014, a massive project was undertaken to revitalise the North Macedonian capital, a controversial makeover that saw large amounts of money pumped into the renewal process. The final result is now the main square of the city and its surroundings, a bold and brash neoclassical collection of pseudo-archaic buildings, more statues than people and all the lights and fountains to embellish them. No one could call it *objectively* beautiful as far as modern city architecture goes, but it's ornate, exciting and it sends a message. It's a controversial space for Macedonians and a polarising one for tourists, but make this your first stop and you will remember the energy of the massive square and the shadow of the impossibly tall Alexander the Great statue – which, for political reasoning, is officially named "equestrian warrior".

Similar buildings line the nearby Vardar river, covering everything from governmental institutions to museums and art galleries. Numerous statues of artists and musicians can be found along the waterside, all adding to the uncanny nature of this part of the city. But the wealth spent on the revitalisation project doesn't quite vibrate out from this epicentre, and that makes Skopje very much a city of two halves, one that mixes modern money with a more typical Balkan vibe.

The Old Bazaar is a must-see, the second largest of its kind in Europe behind Istanbul. Its intertwining and sporadic streets are perfect for the idle explorer, with curios and knicknacks to peruse in every shop window. All of this is in addition to the distinct smells of grilled meats and sweet treats; you'll find grilled kebabs ćevapi on practically every corner and you won't have to look hard for baklava, delicious sweet sheets of pastry layered with chopped nuts and honey. And if you're there at breakfast, live like the locals with a meat- or cheese-stuffed burek pastry and a glass of kefir from any of the numerous bakeries. It's worth tracking down tavče gravče, too, a Macedonian bean-based dish, which you might want to pair with a local rakija, a fermented fruit spirit. To truly indulge in Skopje's historic side, the old Kale Fortress near to the Old Bazaar will offer a glimpse into the Byzantine past as well as a view over Skopje at the highest point of the city.

But Skopje is nothing if not a city break that can provide a variety of things to do, and its nearby natural escapes are close at hand for those who love to be with nature, whether that's a hike (or cable car) to the top of Mount Vodno and its iconic 66-metre (216-feet) crucifix or a 40-minute bus ride to Matka Canyon and the Treska River that has gorged its way through the rugged landscape. However you like your city breaks, Skopje has plenty to remember.

Useful sites
visitskopje.mk
macedonia-timeless.com/events
balkaninsight.com/birn_location/skopje

Essential information

Remember that North Macedonia is a country of political unrest, so it pays to be wary of large crowds or unusual commotion.

Best time to visit Late summer
Currency Ден • Macedonian Denar
Time zone UTC+1

The central stroll along the Vardar river is not a long one, but it's ornate and pleasant

The iconic dual-spire cathedral dominates the skyline of Zagreb, and is perfect for getting your bearings

EAST AND CENTRAL

ZAGREB

CROATIA ISN'T ONLY ABOUT THE BEACH, AND ITS CAPITAL IS MORE THAN ABLE TO PROVE IT...

It's a sad – but perhaps unsurprising – fact that Zagreb is a hard sell when it comes to tourism. Croatia, famed for its gorgeous Dalmatian coastline, UNESCO national parks or the city that doubled as King's Landing, has an abundance of high-quality tourist things to see and do. The problem for Zagreb, then, is its location, hidden away in the northwest corner and a hefty distance from the typical reasons to visit the Adriatic country. But with a history reaching back to further than the late 11th century, as well as a particularly tumultuous modern history, Zagreb has earned itself a lot to say over the centuries.

It's particularly curious because unlike many of the towns and cities that line the coast of Croatia, its architectural influence is less Roman or Venetian – Zagreb is a plethoric mix of styles. Primarily you'll see the Baroque influence of the Habsburg era through much of the lower town, but you'll find elements of Byzantine, Gothic, Renaissance and even Brutalist architecture in and around Zagreb. For city breaks, few places can offer this much variation in buildings. As a city of two halves, the lower town is more akin to its downtown, where its main cultural and shopping areas can be found. The upper town is the older and more historic part of the city, and it's here you'll find many of the main attractions. Notable sites such as St Mark's Church, Mirogoj cemetery, Lotrščak Tower for a rooftop vista and the dual-spired 13th-century cathedral that dominates the skyline of Zagreb are all found here. There's also the Stone Gate, which isn't exactly an enthralling visitors' attraction but still manages to get people making pilgrimages there due to the painting of Virgin Mary that, according to lore, was the only thing that survived from a fire in 1731. The connection between these two halves of the city can be traversed with the shortest funicular in the world. Only taking a little over a minute for it to make its climb, the funicular is more of a novelty than anything else – especially considering the steps that run up alongside it can be taken quicker and still allow you to get a close look at the funicular.

As the cultural and political centre of Croatia for centuries, it's not surprising that Zagreb is also home to a wide number of museums and galleries for those who like to broaden their intellectual horizons during a city break. Explore the options that interest you, but the two unique options are the Museum of Broken Relationships and the Grič Tunnel. The former might surprise you, but the latter – which used to be a World War II evacuation tunnel – is an ever-changing public space for art and exhibitions. If all that sounds a bit much, then Zagreb is also famed for its coffee culture, and it isn't difficult to find any number of coffee shops to suit your tastes. Whether it's a weekend away or as a fly-in destination before heading to the coast, Zagreb has more than enough to tempt you away from the beach.

Useful sites
visitzagreb.hr
np-plitvicka-jezera.hr/en
visit-croatia.co.uk/croatia-destinations/zagreb

Essential information

Zagreb is a great place to base yourself for further trips into mainland Croatia, particularly if you're interested in seeing the iconic Plitvice Lakes.

Best time to visit September is best for warm weather but fewer tourists

Currency Kn • Croatian Kuna

Time zone UTC+1

DUBROVNIK

CROATIA'S STUNNING SEAPORT IS WORTHY OF ITS WORLD-RENOWNED REPUTATION

With its enticing combination of history, culture and coastal scenery, it's no wonder that Dubrovnik has become one of the most popular choices for European holidays in recent years.

Begin your tour of Dubrovnik with a walk along its iconic city walls. The two-kilometre (1.2-mile) stretch provides some of the best views of the Old Town, as well as stunning panoramas of the azure-tinted Adriatic Sea. The first of Dubrovnik's city walls were constructed in the 9th century, with defences being fortified in the 14th century, and forts added to protect against Turkish attacks in the 15th century. These fortresses can be observed as you walk the walls, and your admission ticket will give you access to Fort Lovrijenac, one of the city's most fascinating fortresses and filming location from *Game of Thrones*.

Access to the city walls is granted via two historic gates, Pile and Ploce. Pile is more popular among tourists, so you can get a jump on the crowds by starting your stroll at Ploce. The walk provides little shelter and can be notoriously hot on sunny days, so prepare for scorching weather and take lots of water to avoid overpaying at opportunistic vendors.

Other historic sights to witness in Dubrovnik include Rector's Palace, a Gothic-Renaissance palace that doubles as a cultural history museum; the Franciscan Monastery, which houses a 14th-century pharmacy; and the Large Onofrio's Fountain, which spews drinkable water from the mouths of 16 ornately carved masks.

You can take in the whole city at once from Srd, a 412-metre (1,352-foot) hill that overlooks Dubrovnik and provides unbeatable views of the Old Town, the island of Lokrum and the Elafiti Islands. The easiest and most enjoyable route to the top is via cable car – head up just before sunset to see Dubrovnik at its most enchanting and magical.

Once you're done sightseeing, why not mix things up with a spot of sea kayaking? The activity is a popular pastime in Dubrovnik, and a fun way to get active while enjoying a different perspective of the local scenery. It's easy enough to kayak your way across to the lush island of Lokrum as part of a guided tour. The car-free isle is a popular spot for swimming and provides a tranquil retreat.

All that walking and paddling is hungry work. Luckily enough, Dubrovnik is filled with restaurants that serve some of the best food in Croatia. The specialities here are based on locally caught seafood, and include grilled fish and squid risotto – head to Lokanda Peskarija or Restaurant Proto for some of the best.

For a drink, D'vino offers cosy vibes and an excellent selection of Croatian wine, making it a popular choice, or you can enjoy intoxicating ocean views while sipping beverages at one of two popular cliff-top bars: Buža I and Buža II.

Useful sites
visit-croatia.co.uk/croatia-destinations/dubrovnik
dubrovnikcard.com
www.chasingthedonkey.com

Dubrovnik's well-preserved Old Town is a UNESCO World Heritage Site

Essential information

Buy a Dubrovnik Card for free access to many popular attractions, including the city walls.

Best time to visit April to June
Currency Kn • Croation Kuna
Time zone UTC+1

EAST AND CENTRAL

The Alexander Nevsky cathedral; although it's one of the world's largest orthodox churches, it's recognised for its golden domes

BULGARIA

SOFIA

SOFIA IS A WONDERFUL MIX OF SOVIET ECHOES AND CONTEMPORARY COOL

Sofia is a capital city but it's a small one with a population of just over one million and a geographical size that makes it easy to explore on foot. A city of contrasts, it's a mix of historical gems and youth culture; cool cafes and onion-domed churches; and cold weather and hearty food. In addition, it's youthful, vibrant and affordable and has a very distinctive Soviet vibe.

Even during an initial stroll in the city centre, you see a century-spanning mix of Roman ruins, Soviet buildings, and influence from the Ottoman and Byzantine periods. Visit the city's stunning cathedral, the Alexander Nevsky; it's one of the world's largest orthodox churches and of huge significance to the people of Bulgaria. It was built in the early 1900s to commemorate the fallen soldiers in the Russo Turkish War and is aesthetically notable for its gold domes, marble interior and the mega bells in the tower.

Time-slipping now to the fourth century, you should visit the tiny ex-bathhouse that is Sveti Georgi Rotunda, the oldest building in town, and ogle its magnificent murals from the 13th and 14th centuries. In fact, while you're back in the ancient past, make a trip to Bulgaria's National Museum of History – the perfect way to get a grasp on the country's history. It's divided by era into rooms, with highlights such as antiques from 800 years ago, Thracian gold and Roman artefacts. We also fully recommend making a visit to the Museum of Socialist Art, which shines a light on Bulgaria's years behind the Iron Curtain.

Staying in the more recent past, make sure you check out the National Palace of Culture, an arts events venue that was built in the 1980s to mark the country's 1300th birthday. Hexagonal and huge, the building is a great example of socialist architecture and fans of minimalism and geometric lines will love it.

And now a dip into the arts. There's a great mix of things to do and see in Sofia including the National Gallery Kvadrat 500, an enormous place with a broad mix of exhibits including Bulgarian art from the last two centuries, from headliners like Georgi Mashev and Vladimir Dimitrov, alongside sketches from Renoir and Matisse and African tribal masks. If you're loving the native Bulgarian art, you can indulge yourself further at the Sofia City Art Gallery, which specialises in home-nation paintings as well as sculpture.

Sofia Opera and Ballet, the Sofia Philharmonic Orchestra and the Ivan Vazov National Theatre are great venues for soaking up world-class performances for a fraction of the going ticket price in cultural cities like Milan and Vienna.

All that culture will doubtless work up a thirst that Sofia is more than able to quench. Start with rakia, Bulgaria's national drink, a see-through liquor that is distilled from fruits like grape, apricots and pears. Get yourself down to a Sofian pub like Raketa Rakia Bar for a good selection, but beware – it's strong stuff! If rakia is a bit potent for your tastes, try a mavrud (red wine) with your dinner at Pod Lipite Tavern, which dates back to 1926 and is something of an institution for traditional Bulgarian food.

Useful sites
visitzagreb.hr
np-plitvicka-jezera.hr/en
visit-croatia.co.uk/croatia-destinations/zagreb

Essential information

Sofia has an underground system that connects the airport to the city centre in about 20 minutes.

Best time to visit Late spring, early autumn
Currency ЛB • Bulgarian Lev
Time zone UTC+2

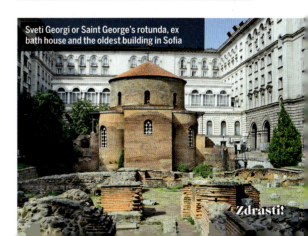

Sveti Georgi or Saint George's rotunda, ex bath house and the oldest building in Sofia

Zdrasti!

ISTANBUL

TURKEY'S CULTURAL CAPITAL LAYS BARE ITS METAMORPHOSIS FROM ROMAN CONQUEST TO MODERN METROPOLIS

Dissected by the glittering Bosphorus strait, separating Europe from Asia, Istanbul is – unlike any other city in the world – a tale of two continents. But its charm is less about East meets West, than new colliding with old.

Founded by the Greeks in the 7th century BC, Istanbul, formerly known as Byzantium, was conquered by the Persians, Athenians, Spartans and Macedonians. It later became the capital of the Roman Empire, when Emperor Constantine rechristened it Constantinople, and remained the capital of the Byzantine Empire for more than 1,000 years, before falling to the Ottoman Turks in 1453.

Luring conquerors and commoners alike, Istanbul's geographic position, straddling two continents, wasn't its only draw – the city also marked the end of the Silk Road. Many a passing merchant loved it so much they decided to stay, weaving a rich cultural tapestry that still exists today, marked into its architectural landscape.

Thanks to its storied past, Istanbul is a living, open-air museum, studded with relics of the great powers who ruled over it – from Roman waterways to extravagant Ottoman estates. This patchwork of historical gems is interrupted with welcome bursts of modern life – contemporary art museums, nightclubs and classic mansions with sleek, glass-fronted extensions. The old quarter's fabled skyline of minarets and domes still sits atop a tangle of narrow, cobbled streets that echo with the muezzin's five daily calls to prayer.

The vestiges of Istanbul's ancient past are mainly dotted around the Sultanahmet district. The opulent pavilions of Topkapı Palace, the administrative seat of the Ottoman Empire for 400 years, stretches behind the magnificent Hagia Sophia (Ayasofya in Turkish). Built by Byzantine emperor Justinian, the basilica was consecrated as a church in 537, before Mehmet II converted it into a mosque in 1453. Atatürk, the father of modern Turkey, later pronounced it a museum.

Gazing across Sultanahmet Square is the iconic Blue Mosque, festooned with 20,000 handcrafted Iznik tiles – famously created from quartz rather than traditional clay. A short stroll northwest, Süleymaniye Mosque crowns one of Istanbul's seven hills, towering over the medieval Grand Bazaar and its labyrinthine maze of coffee shops and stalls – tended by polo-shirt-clad men, balancing spices and loose-leaf tea on brass scales used by their fathers and grandfathers before them.

Just a cheap ferry ride across the Golden Horn, the medieval Galata Tower watches over 'new' Istanbul, and the vibrant entertainment districts of Karaköy, Beyoglu and its namesake Galata – replete with coffee shops, galleries, rooftop bars and boutiques. With cuisine as diverse as its heritage, Istanbul is a food-lover's paradise. Smoky, succulent kebabs, fresh fish and syrupy desserts are best washed down with rakı, the national drink of aniseed brandy, or local wine.

For those who tire of city life, the car-free Princes' Islands, once a safe haven for exiled royal members, are just a 20-kilometre (12-mile) boat trip away. Here, sandy coves and pine forests converge, as horse-drawn carriages with leather seats trundle past seafood restaurants strung along the harbour, hawking the day's catch. A great opportunity to relax.

Useful sites
www.goturkeytourism.com
www.sehirhatlari.istanbul
www.locallyistanbul.com

Essential information

To evade the crowds, visit Topkapı Palace on a Monday morning, and avoid the Hagia Sophia on a Friday.

Best time to visit April to May or September to November

Currency ₺ · Turkish Lira

Time zone UTC+3

Overlooking Sultanahmet Square, the Blue Mosque is adorned with 20,000 handmade Iznik tiles, made from quartz, typically in dark blue, turquoise, emerald and coral

EAST AND CENTRAL

TBILISI

THIS MEDIEVAL CITY IN THE HEART OF THE CAUCASUS IS READY FOR THE FUTURE

Tbilisi, a city whose fiery spirit was once brutally repressed by its Soviet occupiers, is blooming. Georgia is a truly fascinating country, which until a few decades ago, was shut away from the rest of the world. Nowadays, Tbilisi is one of the fastest-growing tourist destinations in Europe. Along the Kura (or in Georgian, Mtkvari) River, fancy hotels, lively nightclubs and world-class restaurants attract locals and tourists alike. Get a feel for Georgia's unique culture and beautiful language as you walk its streets, and listen to the Georgian music coming out of each bar.

The old town is a colourful and exuberant neighbourhood, small enough to explore by foot, but large enough to get serendipitously lost in. Its 19th-century wooden mansions – many featuring elaborate balconies for their owners to people-watch from – are all painted in an array of colours. They might look a little on the 'distressed' side, but it's part of their charm.

In fact, it almost looks like something out of a Disney film – and nowhere is this more apparent than at the Clock Tower. This leaning, higgledy-piggledy tower and its adjacent puppet theatre were built in 2010 by Rezo Gabriadze. Every hour, an angel comes out of the clock to ring the bell, and twice a day you can catch a show in the puppet theatre – we promise it's better than Punch and Judy.

Head out of the Old Town to Rike Park and then look up to the sky. Directly above you, you'll find the imposing Narikala fortress, which has protected the city and the Kura (Mtkvari) River valley since the 4th century. Inside its stone battlements, you can look around a newly restored Eastern Orthodox Church, complete with lavish dome paintings. If you're feeling a touch adventurous, you can walk all the way to the top of the hill – but it's much more fun to take the cable car from Rike Park, which was installed in 2012.

The cable car is just one example of Tbilisi's extensive efforts to modernise and keep pace with other cities in Europe. In another corner of Rike Park, you can find the uber-modern Peace Bridge across the Kura (Mtkvari). Built by the joint efforts of Georgian, French and Italian firms, the bridge symbolises the new Georgia.

But let's not forget that old-fashioned Georgia has its own merits, including the hot sulphur baths. With a constant water temperature of 38 to 40 degrees Celsius (100.4 to 104 degrees Fahrenheit), it's pretty balmy in there – and also a little bit smelly. Don't let that put you off, though. The locals claim the warm, mineral-packed waters will cure a range of ills, from skin conditions to stress to insomnia.

Tbilisi's unique fusion of the old and the new works in perfect harmony with the relaxed Georgian lifestyle. But don't just take our word for it, go and experience it for yourself – this mountainous little country may surprise you.

Useful sites
visitgeorgia.ge/about-georgia/tbilisi/
georgia.travel/
georgiaabout.com/tag/tbilisi/

"They might look distressed, but it's part of their charm"

Essential information

Taxis can try to charge extortionate rates, but public transport is generally efficient, safe and cheap.

Best time to visit May (so you can enjoy the annual Flower Festival)

Currency ₾ · Georgian Lari

Time zone UTC+4

How to get there You can fly into Tbilisi from many bases in Europe and Asia. Alternatively, take the train in from the Armenian capital, Yerevan, or from Azerbaijan's capital Baku

Madloba!

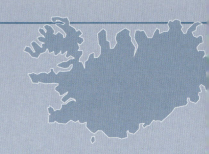

WEST

  94 London
  96 Brighton
  97 Liverpool
  98 York
  99 Manchester
100 Bristol
102 Cardiff
103 Dublin
104 Belfast
105 Edinburgh
106 Stirling
107 Glasgow
108 Amsterdam
110 Rotterdam
111 Bruges
112 Brussels
113 Vienna
114 Salzburg
115 Bern
116 Zurich
117 Hamburg
118 Munich
119 Freiburg Im Breisgau
120 Berlin
122 Luxembourg
123 Nice
124 Paris
126 Lyon
127 Bordeaux
128 Nimes

The Elizabeth Tower is often called Big Ben, but this is in fact the name of the bell

LONDON

FROM RED PHONE BOXES TO BLACK CABS, THERE'S AN ICONIC SIGHT ON EVERY CORNER IN ENGLAND'S CAPITAL CITY

Samuel Johnson once said: "When a man is tired of London, he's tired of life." London is one of the most vibrant cities in the world. It's packed with things to see and do, from beautiful architecture and history to iconic landmarks and, of course, the Royal Family! It's a shopaholic's paradise, a culture vulture's dream and a major foodie hotspot. But beyond this, every neighbourhood has something unique to offer.

Red telephone booths, double-decker buses and the Underground are synonymous with London, but the city is full of iconic sights. One of the most famous landmarks is Big Ben. You can't take a trip to London without taking a photograph in front of the Elizabeth Tower and Houses of Parliament. Mistakenly, most people think Big Ben is the 96-metre (315-foot) clock tower, but it is in fact the massive 13-ton (13,760-kilogram) bell. It's a spectacular sight to see, particularly when lit up at night. Tower Bridge is another landmark that often appears on postcards. One of the city's most famous bridges, its high-level walkways not only offer incredible views of the city, but a different perspective of the River Thames through its glass floor.

There are countless places for epic views, but arguably some of the best vistas can be seen from the London Eye, Europe's largest observation wheel. There is also The View from The Shard; London's tallest building offers the highest viewpoint at 244 metres (800 feet).

If history is what you're after, the Tower of London is the place to visit. This royal palace, fortress and infamous prison encompasses more than 1,000 years of history. Visitors can meet the iconic 'Beefeaters', hear tales of torture and execution, and visit the Crown Jewels at this UNESCO World Heritage Site.

London has three other World Heritage Sites: the Palace of Westminster and Westminster Abbey, Maritime Greenwich, and the Royal Botanic Gardens, Kew. The Palace of Westminster is not only a stunning piece of Victorian Gothic architecture, but it's also home to the Houses of Parliament. Next door, Westminster Abbey is Britain's coronation church and the venue for Prince William and Catherine's wedding.

London has some unique neighbourhoods from affluent Mayfair to bohemian Camden, but the leafy area of Greenwich has some of the best highlights, including the Royal Observatory, National Maritime Museum, Cutty Sark and Greenwich Market. Here you can visit the home of Greenwich Mean Time, see the uniform that Nelson was wearing when he was killed at the Battle of Trafalgar and discover the world's largest surviving tea clipper.

While 30 minutes from the city centre, Kew Gardens highlights its greener side. The world's most diverse collection of living plants is housed here. Hyde Park, Hampstead Heath, Richmond Park, The Regent's Park and St James's Park are just a few of the other green spaces that draw attention to London's natural beauty.

While spring is one of the best times to visit to see London in bloom, if you want a regal day out, you'll have to come in the summer when Buckingham Palace, the King's official London residence, opens to the public. From the Changing of the Guard – a formal ceremony of the King's guards in their red uniforms and bearskin hats – to the 19 lavish stately rooms inside, the palace never fails to impress. Other awe-inspiring palaces include Kensington, the birthplace of Queen Victoria; and Hampton Court, Henry VIII's favourite royal residence. If you still haven't had your royal quota, visit St

Paul's Cathedral to see where King Charles and Diana were married. Climb the 528 steps to the Golden Gallery for spectacular views, or listen to the acoustics in the Whispering Gallery.

Designed by Britain's most famous architect, Sir Christopher Wren, St Paul's is not the only masterpiece. Christ Church at Spitalfields, the Old Painted Hall at the Old Royal Naval College and the St Pancras Renaissance Hotel are all visually astonishing and worth a trip.

London has a plethora of beautiful sights to see, but it's also bursting with things to do. The city is packed with museums and galleries, many of which are free to visit. From the Rosetta Stone at the British Museum to Vincent van Gogh's Sunflowers at The National Galley, it's a treasure trove. Other cultural gems include Tate Modern and Tate Britain, the National Portrait Gallery, the Victoria and Albert Museum, and the Natural History Museum.

Music fans are just as spoilt for choice. Visit the shooting locations for some of the most famous album covers, including the iconic Beatles' *Abbey Road*, or go to top-notch record stores and music venues. Among the best music venues are the Royal Albert Hall, Ronnie Scott's Jazz Club, The Roundhouse in Camden and the O2, which hosts some of the biggest names in music.

But it's not just music and art. London has every form of entertainment from theatre in the West End or at Shakespeare's Globe, to nightclubs, pubs and bars. Have a pint at The George Inn near London Bridge, where Shakespeare once drank, or sip a James Bond martini at DUKES Bar.

Dozens of new bars and restaurants open every month, making the city a holy grail for foodies. From street food to fine dining, there's something for everyone. Visit Brick Lane for a curry, wander Borough Market or take your pick from one of almost 70 Michelin-starred restaurants. If you want the quintessential British experience, have a full English breakfast at a local cafe, enjoy afternoon tea at The Ritz, or eat fish and chips at Poppies.

London is also a fashion capital. From high-end boutiques in Mayfair to flagship stores on Oxford Street, you can shop until you drop. If you're after more than just clothes, Harrods and Fortnum & Mason are almost attractions in their own right, and London's markets, especially Portobello Road, are the perfect place to hunt for unique antiques and one-of-a-kind items.

London has something for everyone. Kids can get a thrill riding the ArcelorMittal Orbit, the world's longest tunnel slide, and sports fans can visit Lord's, Wembley or Wimbledon.

It's such a multicultural city that you can dine on Asian food in Chinatown, watch French cinema at the Barbican, and learn Flamenco at the Southbank Centre all in one day. There are so many events from the Notting Hill Carnival to Chinese New Year. And there's always something different to do. Ride a narrowboat on Regent's Canal, watch street performers in Covent Garden or visit Sherlock Holmes' Baker Street home.

One of the best things about London is that it's ever-changing. You could visit a dozen times and never run out of new things to discover. You may get tired trying to do it all, but like Samuel Johnson, you'll never get tired of London.

Useful sites
www.tfl.gov.uk
www.londonpass.com
www.hrp.org.uk

Essential information

You can buy or top up an Oyster travel card or use a contactless bank card for London transport.

Best time to visit March to May (for mild weather and flowers in bloom) or June to July (for royal palace openings)

Currency £ · Great British Pound

Time zone UTC

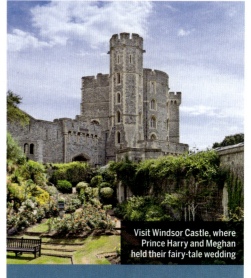
Visit Windsor Castle, where Prince Harry and Meghan held their fairy-tale wedding

FAIRY-TALE VISIT

You can see palaces in London, but if you're making the journey to the UK, you might as well make a trip to one of the best known of them all. Take a day trip to see the world's oldest castle and the venue for two recent royal weddings. Walk in the footsteps of Prince Harry and Meghan Markle or Princess Eugenie and Jack Brooksbank who were both married here.

Windsor Castle is the largest occupied castle, covering 13 acres (five hectares). It is currently one of the Queen's residences, and she spends most of her private weekends here. The castle has more than 900 years of history and has been home to 39 monarchs.

Take an audio tour narrated by King Charles to visit the opulent state rooms and marvel at the Gothic architecture of St George's Chapel. When else will you get to wander a castle?

It's a one-hour train journey from London, but very much worth it for a magical day out.

"You could visit a dozen times and never run out of things to discover"

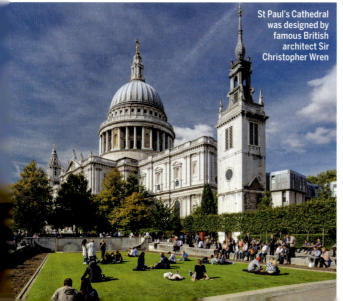
St Paul's Cathedral was designed by famous British architect Sir Christopher Wren

If you want to tour Buckingham Palace, you'll need to visit between the end of July and September

BRIGHTON

DUBBED THE HAPPIEST CITY IN THE UK, BRIGHTON HAS SOMETHING TO PLEASE EVERYONE

Less than an hour away from London (via Victoria Station), the vibrant and eclectic city of Brighton is the perfect choice for those looking for an exciting day trip or a place to spend a few days by the shore.

At its best in the summer, when the skies are blue and the smell of vinegar-soaked fish and chips wafts through the air, Brighton Palace Pier is a staple stop-off for any Brighton visit. Beating wars and ferocious storms to stand tall for 120 years, the pier is both a historical point of interest and an entertainment hub. Spend the afternoon playing games at the arcade, thrill seeking in its dedicated fairground and gorging yourself on authentic British seaside fish and chips. Those interested in more of Brighton's historical offerings should also visit the world's oldest aquarium at SeaLife Brighton and the Royal Pavilion – an Indian-inspired home built for the Prince of Wales in the 18th century.

After getting your fill of the seafront, head down to The Lanes, Brighton's famous maze of narrow alleyways home to a broad range of independent boutiques, jewellers, restaurants and more. Indulge your sweet tooth at Charlie's Sweet Emporium, spend the day reading graphic novels or playing board games at the cosy Dave's Comics, enjoy afternoon tea at That Little Tea Shop in The Lanes, or browse through the samurai swords and other antique weaponry at The Lanes Armoury. For more shopping, make your way to North Laine, where you'll find Oliver's (a haven for *Harry Potter* fans), the eco-friendly Vegetarian Shoes, and Snoopers Paradise, a thrifter's dreamland.

When it comes to food, there's no shortage of excellent eateries to try out. Head over to one of Brighton's oldest pubs, the Lion and Lobster, and enjoy a traditional British dinner made from locally-sourced ingredients. Then there's the lively Proud Cabaret where you can enjoy cabaret, burlesque and drag while eating.

As the Sun sets, stroll around the small city and admire the colourful and unique street art and murals that decorate it, including Banksy's Kissing Policemen (a replica of the original), the Prince Albert pub's music mural (where you'll find paintings of Aretha Franklin, Elvis and Prince to name just a few), rubbish bins painted in homage to the *Star Wars* series and more.

Useful sites
visitsealife.com/brighton
btnbikeshare.com
www.visitbrighton.com

Essential information

Avoid public transport and walk or rent a bike to explore the small city.

Best time to visit May to September for the clearest skies and best temperatures

Currency £ · Great British Pound

Time zone UTC

Brighton Pier was first opened in 1899 and is still a buzzing seaside tourist attraction

Brighton's Royal Pavilion is home to the world's oldest aquarium

WEST

LIVERPOOL

LIVERPOOL IS FAMED FOR ITS MUSICAL HERITAGE, BUT IT ALSO DELIVERS IN TERMS OF HISTORY, CULTURE, SHOPPING AND FOOD

Liverpool is one of those UK cities with a specific energy to it. Whether it's the city's maritime history, the cultural melting pot it became in the 19th century with immigration from the USA, Jamaica and China, the fact that the world's most famous pop band ever grew up and met there, or maybe it's something to do with the scouser's legendary sense of humour... Whatever it is, there's no doubt you'll have a great time in this northern city gem and it's just the right size for a weekend away, with fast train links from all over Britain, particularly London.

First up, why not take to the water in a boat across the Mersey? Yes, it seems like a cliché to follow in the footsteps of Gerry and the Pacemakers, but Liverpool is a city that isn't afraid to milk a cliché, so go for it. You get an excellent feel for the city from the water, too.

Now, there's no way, whatever your age and musical tastes, that you can visit Liverpool without immersing yourself in the Beatles story. There are numerous ways to do this including two attractions (Liverpool Beatles Museum and The Beatles Story) and famous landmarks like Strawberry Field, the childhood homes of the band members, the Beatles sightseeing bus (aka The Magical Mystery tour, of course) and the famous Cavern Club.

Liverpool packs a mean punch in terms of diverse architecture; from the red-brick Albert Dock to the gleaming white Royal Liver Building and the unmissable Liverpool Cathedral. Behind the big sights also lurk many other interesting buildings like the Art Deco Royal Court Theatre, the Cunard HQ and the brownstone warehouses and buildings that can be found around Concert Square.

The cathedral is worth a poke around, not just because of its size. It houses some great art, including large-scale works by the likes of Elizabeth Frink and Tracey Emin. Talking of art, you shouldn't miss the Tate Liverpool at the Albert Dock, which houses a mix of permanent free exhibitions and temporary charged ones. And make time to visit the atmospheric Another Place at Crosby Beach (nine kilometres/six miles from Liverpool), where Gormley's 100 statues stand looking out to sea, at the mercy of the changing tides.

Half the charm of Liverpool lies in its diversity; you get the feeling you can be anything there and everyone will be welcomed with open arms (apart from a Man U supporter maybe!). This vibe trickles into all parts of life, including music, the arts, gastronomy and even shopping; for instance, you can go wild in the aisles of Liverpool ONE, the UK's largest open air shopping centre, or stick to the iconic vintage stores and indie retailers of Bold Street. Or you can do both – it's up to you!

Useful sites
visitliverpool.com
liverpoolpass.co.uk
liverpoolbeatlesmuseum.com

Essential information

When you're footsore and hungry, you should try Duke Street Market, home to six different kitchens and cuisines.

Best time to visit All year round
Currency £ · Great British Pound
Time zone UTC

Immerse yourself in the story of the Fab Four while you're in their hometown

The wonderful Antony Gormley sculptures on Crosby Beach just north of the city

"There's no doubt you'll have a great time in this northern city gem"

ENGLAND

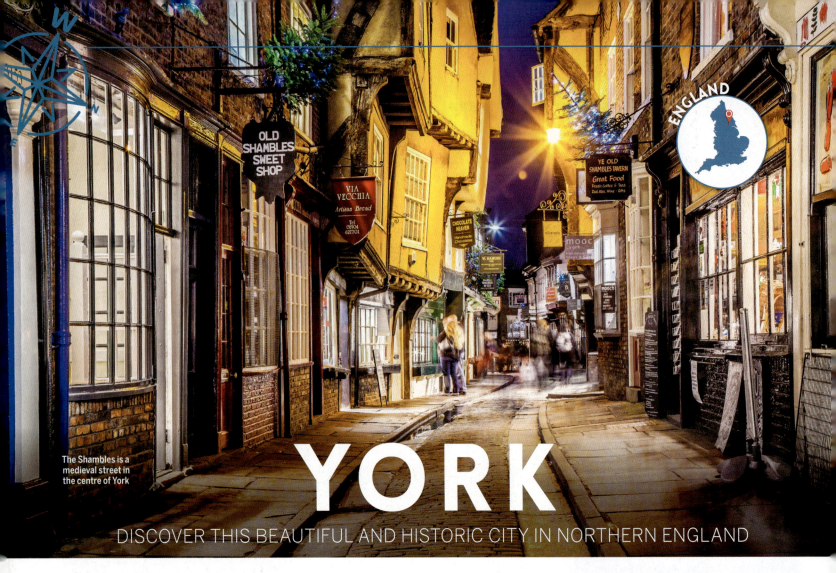

The Shambles is a medieval street in the centre of York

YORK

DISCOVER THIS BEAUTIFUL AND HISTORIC CITY IN NORTHERN ENGLAND

As soon as you set foot in the charming city of York, you will realise just how special it is. It dates back almost 2,000 years and is bursting with history and culture. The city was founded by the ancient Romans, who named it Eboracum, in 71 CE. Even though there is not much left from that time period today, the Roman Fortress wall is one of the city's most iconic sights and a great place to start your visit.

Despite the fact that the Romans left their mark on the city, York is undoubtedly most associated with the Vikings, who invaded the city in 866 and gave it the new name, Jorvik. Today, York widely celebrates its Viking past, and links to its Norse heritage can be found everywhere. A visit to the immersive Jorvik Viking Centre is perfect for any history buffs who want to take a step back in time and learn what everyday life was like for the Vikings.

If the Jorvik Centre is not Viking enough for you, then make sure you plan your trip for February, so that you can attend the annual Jorvik Festival. The largest Viking festival in Europe, the festival includes walking tours, expert talks, craft workshops, market stalls, as well as living history events.

Aside from the city's Viking links, it is impossible to walk around York and not notice the sheer beauty of its architecture. The city is home to York Minster, which is not only one of the largest cathedrals in Northern Europe, but is also a breathtaking example of Gothic architecture. Meanwhile, Clifford's Tower, the medieval fortress that has recently been refurbished with new walkways, stairways and a new roof deck, offers visitors stunning panoramic views of the city and is just a 15-minute walk from the cathedral.

Of course, a trip to York simply wouldn't be complete without a visit to the iconic Shambles. One of the best-preserved medieval streets in Europe, with overhanging buildings and cobbled stress, the Shambles is home to a number of York's independent businesses including The York Ghost Merchants, a popular souvenir shop amongst tourists.

Speaking of ghosts, York is considered to be one of the world's most haunted cities. If you like bloody tales of gore, murder and more, then take one of the many eerie ghost tours that the city has to offer – these walking tours are ideal for those with limited time who still want to see as much of the city as possible.

York is also a dream destination for food lovers, serving up delicious cuisines from all over the world. Whether you're looking for a casual lunch spot, a cosy family-run cafe, or upscale dining, the city has something to offer everyone. You can find a variety of stalls serving delicious street food at the Shambles Market, which is ideal for people who are always on the go. If you have a sweet tooth, a trip to York's Chocolate Story is a must. Here, you can discover the city's rich history with chocolate and indulge in some delectable treats.

Whether you want to step back in time or into the world of chocolate, behind every door in York, a new world awaits you.

Essential information

It is much easier to get around the centre of York by foot than by car.

Best time to visit All year round
Currency £ · Great British Pound
Time zone UTC

Useful sites
visityork.org
makeityork.com
jorvikvikingcentre.co.uk

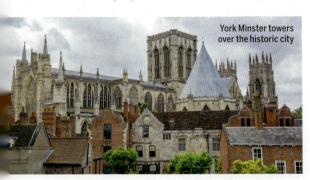

York Minster towers over the historic city

WEST
MANCHESTER

A CULTURAL HOTSPOT IN NORTHERN ENGLAND, WHERE GALLERIES, MUSIC VENUES AND MUSEUMS BREAK ALL THE RULES

Creative, cosmopolitan and genuinely welcoming, Manchester marches to the beat of its own drum. Today, the city that gave birth to the computer, socialism and votes for women, teems with cultural and historic gems, world-class restaurants and, of course, a legendary music scene.

Culture begins at Manchester Art Gallery, which houses an extensive collection of British and European art by the likes of Cézanne, Renoir, Turner and Lowry. For those short on time, the gallery runs free hour-long tours from Thursday to Sunday. Further south, emerging from a sprawling urban park, the Whitworth Art Gallery displays a magnificent selection of work by contemporary artists, including Degas, Picasso, Freud and Hockney. It also plays host to the Art Garden, created by celebrated landscape designer, Sarah Price.

Across town, the Science and Industry Museum traces the city's rich industrial legacy through a series of immersive exhibitions, while the People's History Museum charts the country's colourful political past, and its journey to democracy.

Meanwhile, literary buffs can explore Chetham's Library. Founded in 1653, it's the oldest public library in the English-speaking world and was once the meeting place for Marx and Engels – the desk where the duo researched their ideas for The Communist Manifesto still remains. A short walk south lies the John Rylands Library, its neo-Gothic turrets and grand arches rising gracefully above a sea of ultra-modern steel and glass. Inside, its dimly lit innards open into a cavernous reading room, overlooked by stained glass and marble statues of literary giants. The library even houses a fragment of New Testament writing, believed to be the earliest ever found.

Just 1.6 kilometres (one mile) east, the cobbled streets of the Northern Quarter unfold in a maze of independent shops, laid-back cafes and vinyl stores. While Oi Polloi offers up a cool edit of street-inspired menswear, Magma stocks an eclectic mix of photography and design books, and niche magazines.

Come nightfall, the city's legendary music scene proves it is alive and well. Musicians take to the stage at Matt & Phred's, an unpretentious but achingly cool jazz bar, serving up food and drink six nights a week. On the city's outskirts, experiential music venues abound, like Hidden – a labyrinthine club set across three floors of a former mill – The Deaf Institute, as well as the White Hotel.

If pumping beats don't entice, the seasonally minded, local fare at Michelin-star restaurant, Mana, certainly will. In the area of Ancoats, Rudy's serves up the best pizza in the city, thanks to its double-fermented dough and Neapolitan ingredients. Elsewhere, neon-drenched Chinatown throbs with specialist bakeries, dim-sum dens and karaoke bars.

Useful sites
visitmanchester.com
library.chethams.com
scienceandindustrymuseum.org.uk

Essential information

While Manchester's city centre is walkable, a free bus, the Metroshuttle, loops around the city centre.

Best time to visit June and August, for warm weather and a busy events calendar

Currency £ · Great British Pound

Time zone UTC

Nicknamed 'Cottonopolis' in the 19th century, Manchester was one of the world's first industrial cities

ENGLAND

BRISTOL

THE CULTURAL CAPITAL OF THE BRITISH SOUTHWEST

The city of Bristol in England's proud West Country has a history ranging back over 1,000 years as a trading hub, its network spanning all the way from French Gascony to far-flung Iceland during the Middle Ages. A vital port and industrial centre for a long time, it quickly reinvented itself as a cultural hub in the late-20th century as its heavy industry faded. In the 21st century, without much fanfare, Bristol has become a centre for creative arts, music and theatre, with an impressive number of live-music venues, museums, galleries and theatres for a city of its easily walkable size.

After years of operating under the radar, today Bristol is an up-and-coming destination for any travellers looking for a variety of activities, events and days out. You can go down to the old docks and board the innovative SS Great Britain steamship. The brainchild of Isambard Kingdom Brunel, the godfather of the Industrial Revolution, the SS Great Britain was the first great ocean liner when it was launched in 1843. In the 1970s it was saved from becoming scrap metal, restored to its former glory and turned into what's now Bristol's most popular attraction. Board the boat to experience life above and below deck, or watch one of the many interactive performances happening in the dry dock.

Another fantastic, unique museum experience is Aerospace Bristol, which

Essential information

 The water's edge (i.e. the Harbourside) is your best bet for a fun-filled day full of experiences.

Best time to visit July has good weather and something happening most days, or August for the annual Balloon Fiesta

Currency £ · Great British Pound

Time zone UTC

How to get there A two-hour train ride from London, Bristol also has its own international airport

WEST

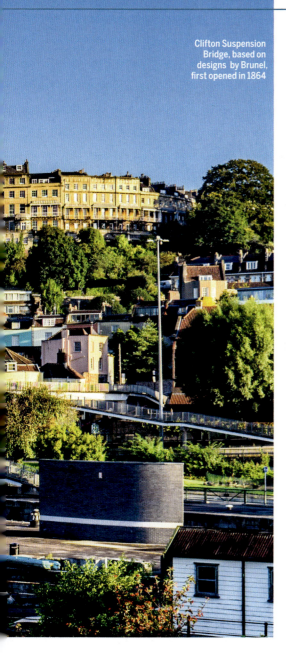

Clifton Suspension Bridge, based on designs by Brunel, first opened in 1864

Works by the elusive Banksy are a common sight on the streets of Bristol

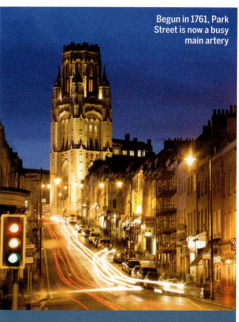

Begun in 1761, Park Street is now a busy main artery

highlights and celebrates Bristol's world-leading aerospace industry. Aerospace Bristol's crown jewel is an actual Concorde jet on display, the first-ever supersonic passenger jet that ferried travellers between the UK and the USA in style until 2003.

You'll see links to Bristol's industrial past everywhere you go, but it doesn't mean the city dwells there. Over the last four decades, in the spirit of its previous industrial innovation, Bristol has made a name for itself as a hotbed for trail-blazing musical and artistic creation, from world-famous, genre-defining musical acts in the 1990s like Portishead, Roni Size and Massive Attack to innovative emerging acts of today like Idles and Blanck Mass. Finding a memorable night out in Bristol to see great original live acts is easy, and so is finding live performance of other kinds.

The Bristol theatre and dance scene is bigger now than ever before. Established theatres like the Bristol Old Vic always have ambitious productions on, and a number of venues host independent artists. Some of the most interesting include The Tobacco Factory, where everything from child-friendly family shows to progressive dance-theatre productions are on offer, and the Arnolfini, which hosts a fantastic art gallery. Then there's the Watershed located on the Harbourside, a digital media centre that hosts independent film screenings, music and theatre performances and design and visual art installations.

One of the biggest events every year in Bristol is St. Paul's Carnival, which has been held yearly since 1968 and grown into a cross-cultural coming together of Bristol's diverse population. Established to celebrate Afro-Caribbean culture and its influence on modern Bristol, today St. Paul's Carnival is held on the first Saturday of July and incorporates a massive musical procession where people enjoy an upbeat, vibrant community spirit. In fact, Bristol has live outdoor events going on throughout most of the year. From public parks to the Harbourside and even event-hosting cemeteries, you'll be able to find pop-up performances, live music shows and interactive attractions to suit any taste.

Days out can include excursions to historic castles on the outskirts of the city, busy Bristol Zoo and to see Bristol's historic bridges across the Avon, including the engineering marvel that is the Clifton Suspension Bridge. The Clifton neighbourhood, in fact, is ideal for history lovers – its golden buildings represent the city's wealthy past (many of which were built on the backs of slavery and colonialism), and there are lots of cobbled streets and green squares to enjoy walks in. Royal York Crescent is a great alternative to the Georgian city streets of Bath, and it offers panoramic views over the entire Bristol area.

PARK STREET

If you're mooching around the City Centre, chances are you'll be able to look up and see the fire-hose shaped Wills Memorial Building of Bristol University. This grand, golden tower is a true landmark, sitting on a vantage point atop a hill. You can get even higher by taking a tour to the top of the tower every Saturday.

To get there you'll want to wander up one of the city's best shopping streets: Park Street. Start at College Green, where you can enjoy a delicious gelato and brioche sandwich. It faces onto the historic Bristol Cathedral, which is worth a look if you have the time.

As you go uphill, you can browse vintage clothes shops, stop off in a chocolate cafe, or even buy some eco-friendly homeware from one of the many quirky furniture retailers.

When you reach the top, you'll be able to look down towards the city, admire Bristol University, or continue on to one of the lively bars of Whiteladies Road.

The city centre has been massively renovated in recent years. Gone are the days of 1960s squalor – you'll find shiny new shopping centres, towering office blocks, and quirky side alleys. Climb up the Christmas Steps to explore niche boutiques and bookshops, or enjoy a meal at the Harbourside's plethora of restaurants. To experience an edgier part of town, take a walk through the infamous Bearpit subway and stroll up Stoke's Croft – there are vintage shops, curry houses and Banksy artworks galore.

Useful sites
visitbristol.co.uk
ssgreatbritain.org
bristolmuseums.org.uk

Built in 2004 and found at the forefront of Roald Dahl Plass, the Millennium Centre was fashioned entirely from materials sourced from Wales

Essential information

For more excitement, visit during rugby seasons when the atmosphere is electric.

Best time to visit June to September
Currency £ · Great British Pound
Time zone UTC

CARDIFF

TV BUFFS, BOOKWORMS, SPORTS FANS AND HISTORY LOVERS UNITE IN THE COLOURFUL WELSH CAPITAL

For those who thrive off of the buzz of city life, Wales's capital city is the place to go. Not only is Cardiff a multicultural hub, steeped in history and Welsh heritage, but it is also a lively region brimming with lots of amazing things to see and do.

Top of any tourist's list of 'places to visit' is Cardiff Bay. Less than 100 years ago, the area was a stopgap for numerous ships that docked in the port, but in more recent years it has been transformed into a beautiful meeting point with a great selection of bars and restaurants, as well as a stunning view across the waters. Boat tours promise a panoramic view of the beauty of the bay and its iconic sights such as the Pierhead, the Norwegian Church, old docks and Wetlands Nature Reserve. Around the corner from the former docks, and just a stone's throw from the impressive Millennium Centre (where you can catch your favourite playwrights and musicians) is Roald Dahl Plass, which as well as being dedicated to the famous Cardiff-born author, is home to many of the fantastic events that are hosted throughout the year in the city. Not only is Roald Dahl Plass steeped in heritage, it is also famous for hosting the cast of popular sci-fi series such as *Dr Who* and *Torchwood* – its tall metallic statue might even look familiar to Torchwood fans, who will recognise it as the secret entrance to the show's infamous HQ.

Away from the bay is the stunning Cardiff

Once owned by the noble Bute family, Cardiff Castle now provides visitors with a stunning backdrop to their Cardiff adventure

Castle. One of the city's most famous attractions for the last few decades, the 2,000-year-old building can be found in the heart of the city. It is also surrounded by the beautiful Bute Park, which is perfect for a summer's day walk and delivers a truly peaceful experience. The castle was owned by the noble Bute Family until after the death of the fourth Marquess, John Crichton-Stuart, in 1947, when it and most of its gardens were gifted to the city. As well as offering access to the grounds and exhibits, the castle also features a Norman keep and bomb shelters used in World War II. Neaby, Cardiff's Museum, which opened in 1922, is one of several National Museum of Wales sites across the country and provides an unfettered view of the city throughout its history. With so much to see and do in Wales's capital city, it comes as no surprise that Cardiff is popular all year round.

Useful sites
www.visitcardiff.com
www.cardiffbay.co.uk
www.cardiffcastle.com

WEST

REPUBLIC OF IRELAND

DUBLIN

ENJOY GUINNESS, LIVE MUSIC AND GREAT CRAIC IN IRELAND'S LIVELY CAPITAL

It may have a reputation of not being the prettiest of cities, but Dublin has so much to offer. Even on the darkest and dreariest of days, Dublin will still thrive – you just need to know the right places to go.

If you only have a few days, then we'd recommend that you try one of the hop-on, hop-off bus tours, as they are a great way to see a lot of the city very quickly. You can ride the whole circuit in one go or get off at one of the many tourist hotspots. Popular stops include the Guinness Storehouse, Kilmainham Gaol, Dublin Zoo, Temple Bar, Trinity College, Grafton Street, O'Connell Street, where the tour begins, and many more.

A trip to Dublin wouldn't be complete without a tour of the Guinness Storehouse. Even if you aren't keen on the drink itself, the stunning, panoramic views of the city from the top-floor Gravity Bar will make your visit worthwhile. Discover everything there is to know about Guinness across the exhibits of the seven-floored converted grain house, from its history to how it is made today.

Wander along the banks of the River Liffey and walk across one of its 24 bridges in Greater Dublin, the most famous of which being the Ha'penny Bridge – the Liffey's first pedestrian crossing, dating back to 1816. Like the Pont des Arts in Paris, the Ha'penny has seen a spell of 'love locks' being attached to the famous railings by loved-up couples, although this has proven to be detrimental to the structure.

Another worthwhile place to visit is Kilmainham Gaol, a prison which first opened its doors to prisoners in 1796 and shut in 1924. The site is steeped in Dub dark history – see the courtyard where prisoners met their fates by firing squad, or the gallows where they were hanged for their crimes. Today, the Gaol is seen as a symbol of Irish Nationalism, as many of the leaders from the rebellion of 1798 and the Irish Civil War of 1922-23 were detained here.

Temple Bar is where you should head on an evening if you fancy some lively nightlife – it is *the* spot for a tipple and a jig. Though the area is famous for attracting stag and hen parties, the atmosphere in the many bars and pubs remains friendly. If you don't squeeze yourself into a pub that has standing room only, to listen (or sing along) to live traditional Irish music with a drink in your hand, then you may as well have stayed at home.

Useful sites
www.dublinpass.com
www.discoverireland.ie/visit-dublin
www.dublinvisitorcentre.ie

"Temple bar is where you should head if you fancy a tipple and a jig"

The Temple Bar Pub has traditional live music seven days a week

Essential information

Sample Dublin's oysters with a pint of Guinness.
Best time to visit All year round
Currency € · Euro
Time zone UTC

Dia duit!

BELFAST

FROM THE TITANIC TO THE TROUBLES, BELFAST HAS AN INTERESTING PAST JUST WAITING TO BE UNCOVERED

Say Belfast, say mini break, right? If Belfast isn't top of your list of weekend destinations, you're a bit [whispers] behind the times, because the city has gone through a transformation in recent years and it's now a hip, cultural and beautiful place to visit with a fascinating and thought-provoking past to explore.

The Titanic was built in Belfast and set sail from the city's dock on that fateful day in 1912. Now the Titanic slipways, the Harland and Wolff Drawing Offices and the Hamilton Graving Dock, the places where the Titanic was designed, built and launched, have been turned into a visitor experience that tells the story of the ship, its creation, its passengers and workers and, of course, its ill-fated voyage. Expect a self-guided tour, interactive galleries, full-scale reconstructions and special effects.

Second on your list of historical must-dos is more recent but equally infamous. It's over 20 years since the end of the Troubles, but the scars are still fresh in hearts and minds of locals so it's with a great deal of sensitivity that a trend for 'Troubles Tourism' has now sprung up in the city.

There are many walking, cycling and taxi tours to choose from, with subject matters ranging from a general view of Belfast's history to talks by former political prisoners sharing their personal experiences. One fascinating and emotive way to explore the city's past is by touring the Peace Walls, the walls between the Falls and Shankill Roads that used to divide warring groups. They remain intact and are now painted with commemorative art and slogans for peace, but are still separated by the ugly metal gates that were used as security checkpoints. A stark reminder of times past and the 3,500 lives lost to the conflict.

A recent addition to Belfast's touristic armoury is *The Game of Thrones* Studio Tour. Northern Ireland was dubbed 'Home of Thrones' from the start of the small-screen phenomenon and was the location for 25 scenes. Rather like the *Harry Potter* Studio Tour in Watford, die-hard fans take a self-guided tour through sets, costumes, props and set pieces and immerse themselves in the *GoT* universe. Tickets include a shuttle bus from Belfast centre – the journey is 40 kilometres (25 miles).

There's so much more to do in Belfast – namely Crumlin Road Gaol, C S Lewis Square, Belfast City Hall, the Botanic Gardens and The Ulster Museum, which combines art, history and natural history under one roof. But we're focussing on food, namely the wonderful St George's Market. It's a renovated covered market and it's at its most vibrant on Friday, Saturday and Sunday mornings. The traders sell everything from fresh seafood to soda bread to local goat meat and of course, an Ulster Fry. Belfast is home to a burgeoning gastronomic scene; look out for Michelin-starred options, EIPIC, OX, and The Muddlers Club, as well as Deanes at Queens and Home, both recipients of the Bib Gourmand.

Useful sites
ireland.com
visitbelfast.com
titanicbelfast.com

Belfast City Hall in Donegall Square in the city centre

The street art that now adorns many of the walls that used to separate parts of Belfast during the Troubles is a moving tribute and reminder of past pain

The Titanic Museum is a wonderful addition to Belfast's tourist offering

"The city has gone through a transformation in recent years"

Essential information

Belfast Visitor Pass is very reasonable (£6 per day) and includes transport as well as reduced entry to certain attractions.

Best time to visit Late spring and early summer are driest

Currency £ · Great British Pound

Time zone UTC

Dia dhuit!

EDINBURGH

THE PICTURESQUE CAPITAL CITY HAS SOMETHING FOR EVERYONE – FROM HISTORICAL ATTRACTIONS TO THRIVING FESTIVALS

Arguably the best city in Scotland, this beautiful capital is absolutely steeped in history. The iconic Edinburgh Castle sits in pride of place in the middle of the city centre on top of an extinct volcano – completely dominating the skyline. You have to visit the castle on the rock, even if only to recognise the pivotal role that it played in Scottish history. In 1058, it became a royal residence and a military stronghold for King Malcolm Canmore and later Queen Elizabeth. The castle today is one of Scotland's most popular and atmospheric tourist attractions. In August, book tickets for the Royal Edinburgh Military Tattoo, which takes place on the castle's esplanade.

Explore the city's spooky past by embarking on an adventure underground to the city beneath the city, and delve into 400 years of history at the Real Mary King's Close. During the day, enjoy a historical tour about the close and warren of streets, homes and passageways and unlock the secrets of Edinburgh's buried past. Learn the eerie myths and stories about those who lived in the city and tall tenement buildings, visit the butcher's shop and find out about the plague that swept across the city. Or if you are brave enough, take the late-night Tales of Witchcraft and Misadventure tour for a darker and more dramatic look at Edinburgh's volatile past.

During the month of August, Edinburgh transforms into a hub of culture, comedy and fun. Experiencing the city during the festival is a must – the Edinburgh International Festival and the Edinburgh Fringe Festival run alongside each other. The Old Town fills with street performers, comedy shows, arts and theatre, and the bars stay open later. The city thrives during August and welcomes tourists from all over the world with open arms.

To get an unusual and unique view of the city, visit Camera Obscura, or learn about how life on Earth evolved at Dynamic Earth. If you're brave enough, climb the 288 stairs up to the Scott Monument for an impressive view of Princes Street, the gardens, the Old Town and the castle, or head to Edinburgh Zoo, which is home to the only knighted penguin in the world, Sir Nils Olav, as well as two giant pandas, which both make the zoo worth visiting.

You can't visit the capital without going into one of the many tartan shops to try on a kilt, or a whiskey shop and sampling one of the delicious malts. If whiskey isn't your thing, try the Edinburgh Gin Distillery for a taste of the multi-award-winning small-batch spirit.

Useful sites
www.edinburgh.org
www.visitscotland.com
www.realmarykingsclose.com

Essential information

Buses now accept contactless payment, for stress-free travel around the city.

Best time to visit August for the festival
Currency £ · Great British Pound
Time zone UTC

The majestic Edinburgh Castle dominates the city's skyline

STIRLING

THIS SMALL CITY IS STEEPED IN SCOTTISH HISTORY, AND IS WELL WORTH THE TRIP

When you think of Scotland, you'll likely conjure up images of Edinburgh Castle, but many forget about the city of Stirling, its castle and the crucial part it played in the history of Scotland.

Stirling is home to many secret Scottish gems not to be missed. The city is roughly equidistant between Edinburgh and Glasgow, so you have no excuse not to go.

To the untrained eye, Stirling Castle looks like Edinburgh Castle's younger sibling. Like Edinburgh, Stirling Castle sits proudly at the centre of the city on a rocky cliff. Inside the castle walls, you'll find the Royal Palace, which now frequently hosts an exciting world of plots, passion and intrigue with costumed performers bringing history to life. You'll also find a new exhibition focused on the castle's archaeology, which includes the fascinating, mysterious 14th-century Stirling skeletons. Other highlights include the Great Hall, Chapel Royal, Regimental Museum, the great kitchens as well as dress up, games and musical instruments to keep younger visitors entertained.

The next thing you can't leave without seeing is the National Wallace Monument, a tower built in memory of the Scottish hero, Sir William Wallace. Inside you'll find The Hall of Arms that shows how the battle of Stirling Bridge against the English king was fought and won, as well as information on the life of William Wallace. Also found inside is The Hall of Heroes, a celebration of famous Scots who were inspired by Wallace and home to the Wallace sword as well as the facts and figures behind the building of the monument in The Royal Chamber.

If none of that has enticed you, then simply go for the views. Seriously. On one side you'll see the city itself, Stirling Bridge, the Forth river and the castle perched in pride of place on a hill. When it's been snowing the hills around the city make the most stunning backdrop. On the other side you'll see Stirling University Campus, which is a campus like no other. In the centre of the university grounds there's a beautiful loch that freezes over in the winter months and glistens for the rest of the year, and is home to swans, ducks and other wildlife.

Behind the campus is Dumyat Hill, a rocky little hill of the Ochils range, which is worth the climb if you have time. You might hear stories about the Sheriffmuir Inn (off the hill path) that used to be home to a friendly grizzly bear... but we're not sure how credible these tales are.

Other highlights include the Old Town Jail, The Church of the Holy Rude, The Battle of Bannockburn Experience, and Argyll's lodging.

Useful sites
yourstirling.com/see-do/top-attractions/
stirlingcitypass.com/

Essential information

 Pack your anorak and walking boots, as impromptu hikes are essential to any Scotland visit.

Best time to visit July and August – Scottish winters are chilly!

Currency £ · Great British Pound

Time zone UTC

Time zone Hop on a train from Edinburgh or Glasgow right to the centre of Stirling.

"Stirling Castle sits proudly at the centre of the city on a rocky cliff"

Essential information

🏴󠁧󠁢󠁳󠁣󠁴󠁿 For a great view, go to the Necropolis. It sits on a hill next to Glasgow Cathedral.

Best time to visit April-August

Currency £ · Great British Pound

Time zone UTC

GLASGOW

FOR CULTURE, CHARM AND A WARM ATMOSPHERE, LOOK TO VISIT GLASGOW, SCOTLAND'S LARGEST CITY

At one time it was a hub for importing and trade for the UK, but today Glasgow is a hub for arts and culture. Many may know Edinburgh as being a cultural hotspot due to the Fringe Festival but Glasgow is really the place to be as there is always something on. One of the best things about Glasgow is that you don't need to leave the city centre to experience all it has to offer. Museums, green spaces, street art and music venues are all available from the centre of Glasgow.

The Style Mile is Glasgow's shopping district where you can look around worldwide brands and independent stores. While browsing Sauchiehall Street you should visit the Willow Tearooms. Designed by architect Charles Rennie Mackintosh, it presents an experience for all the senses. A ten-minute walk from there takes you to the Tenement House and back in time to the early 20th century. From the outside, the National Trust site looks like any other tenement property in the city, but the inside remains as a time capsule. Get an authentic look at house life of Glasgow in the 1900s as it has been untouched in over 60 years.

While still in the city centre, go to the Gallery of Modern Art, the city's most visited museum, helped in part by the statue of the Duke of Wellington that sits just outside. Locals have been putting traffic cones on the head of the Duke for years and it shows the character of the locals. It is often said that "People make Glasgow" and it is true.

Although known for the oddity that is the deep-fried Mars bar, Glasgow has countless good spots for food and drinks. If you're vegan or vegetarian then you will have no issues finding somewhere as more independent businesses open catering to all diets. Micro breweries are dotted around the city or you can check out Tennent's brewery tour.

If you decide to explore beyond the city centre, getting around is a breeze with the numerous modes of transport; Bike rentals, buses, trains and a subway are all available. The easiest way of getting from the city centre to the west end or south is the subway, sometimes called the Clockwork Orange due to the colour of the trains. This underground system goes in a loop around the city. A short metro or bus journey away from the city centre is The Kelvingrove Art Gallery and Museum. A must-see spot, it is free to enter and see the extraordinary exhibits including, most notably, *Christ of Saint John of the Cross* by Salvador Dali. If live music is your thing then you will be spoilt for choice. King Tut's Wah Wah Hut has housed many upcoming bands but the Barrowland Ballroom is unforgettable with its large neon sign on the front and spring floor.

Useful sites
peoplemakeglasgow.com
visitscotland.com
glasgowconventionbureau.com

Erected in 1844, this statue of the Duke of Wellington is one of Glasgow's most iconic sights

AMSTERDAM

UNCOVER THIS BEAUTIFUL CANAL CITY IN THE HEART OF THE NETHERLANDS

As you disembark the train at Amsterdam Centraal and make your way to the front of the beautiful 19th-century building, there's a whole city full of history and culture waiting to be explored. Perhaps you've got a week, or maybe just a short weekend break, it doesn't matter – there's more than enough to keep you occupied. The most difficult decision you'll have is where to go first.

It's probably important to get the lay of the land first, and while a map can be great for this, there's a better option. Once you've left Amsterdam Centraal, head left and take a walk along Stationsplein and then Oosterdokskade until you come across Openbare Bibliotheek Amsterdam. While this is the city library, there's a restaurant on the top floor with a balcony that provides stunning views of Amsterdam on a clear day, with a handy map of the skyline. You'll be able to spot both Oude Kerk and Nieuwe Kerk (churches), and admire the traditional Dutch gable houses that make Amsterdam so iconic.

The first tourist destination most people head to is Dam Square, and there's a reason for that. While it has a Madame Tussauds on one side, it's also home to the Nationaal Monument and, perhaps more excitingly, Amsterdam's royal palace, Koninklijk Paleis. Entrance to the palace is only about £8.60 ($11) for adults, and it's a chance to take a walk through the Netherlands' rich royal history. Dam Square is also near to the Red Light District, which highlights the liberal culture of the city and is certainly worth a visit.

But Amsterdam's past isn't only known for its royalty – the city used to be home to artists aplenty, and a trip to Museumplein (Museum Square) is a must for any art or art-history lover. Dominating the area is the Rijksmuseum, a Dutch national museum that houses works created by Rembrandt and Vermeer, among others. Of course, a quick stroll past the water feature (which incidentally is perfect to dip your feet into on a hot day) will find you at the Van Gogh Museum, which holds the largest collection of Van Gogh paintings in the world. However, if modern art is more your style, then take a trip to the nearby Stedelijk Museum.

Of course, Amsterdam also has a darker history, and the person probably most famously associated with it is Anne Frank. The youngest in a Jewish family, she, her sister and her

The Anne Frank House can have long queues, so it's worth booking your slot ahead of time

You'll find cheese shops all over the city, and many offer free samples

parents fled Nazi Berlin for Amsterdam. When the Nazis invaded the Netherlands, they went into hiding in an attic on Prinsengracht, but they were betrayed a few years later. After being sent to concentration camps, only Anne's father, Otto, survived. The attic is now open to the public, and walking through the concealed entrance to the hiding space is a harrowing experience. The floorboards creak underfoot – it's hard to imagine how still the family and their fellow fugitives had to stay to avoid detection.

There's more to Amsterdam than its history. The lifeblood that flows through the city are the canals, arranged in an ever-expanding horseshoe. There are plenty of companies running boat tours up and down the canals, and it's a great opportunity to see some of the beautiful Dutch architecture, as well as scope out where you want to go next. But connecting all the canals is the Amstel, the river after which the beer is named. If you're after a little of the beverage, head over to the Heineken Experience on Stadhouderskade for a tour of the brewery and a tasting at the end.

One thing you'll spot a lot of are the cheese shops – it seems like they're on every corner.

> *"Admire the Dutch gable houses that make Amsterdam so iconic"*

Be sure to jump on a bike to see the real Amsterdam

WEST

Amsterdam is known for its architecture and beautiful canals

If you want a gift to take home to family and friends, this is perfect. Inside you'll find brightly wrapped Dutch cheeses that are smoked, infused with pesto and more. You'll also be able to buy your stroopwafels here – caramel waffles that go very well with a good cup of coffee.

That brings us to food. You'll find every type of cuisine imaginable here – it's a city, after all – but it can be good to stray a little from the centre of the city where things are geared more towards tourists. Out in the suburbs you can eat like a local, although central Amsterdam will still be good for your crêpes, fries and bagels.

If you're eating on the go, or you'd just like a break from the hustle and bustle of the city, Amsterdam is more than ready to provide. Dotted around the city you'll find glorious parks, each offering a slice of peace. The most famous is probably Vondelpark, in the southeast, and it has some beautiful small lakes. You may even stumble upon a free concert in the spring or summer months. Elsewhere, there's Rembrandtpark (near Rembrandtplein), Westerpark, Amstelpark and Oosterpark, as well as ARTIS, Amsterdam's zoo.

If you somehow run out of things to do in Amsterdam, there's no need to worry – the city is well connected, and you can jump on a train and head all over the country. The Hague is only half an hour or so away, along with Rotterdam, Dordrecht and Utrecht. You can also head over the border and into Germany or Belgium, which can come in handy if you're wanting to embark on a tour of Europe. But Amsterdam is a beautiful city, and there's so much to do there that filling your holiday shouldn't be all that difficult. With culture, history and food aplenty, you're bound to leave feeling like you're flying high.

Useful sites
www.iamsterdam.com/en
www.amsterdampass.com
www.en.gvb.nl/amsterdam-travel-ticket

Essential information

Be careful when walking in Amsterdam – bikes can appear in front of you out of nowhere!

Best time to visit All year round
Currency € • Euro
Time zone UTC+1

Trams run all over the city centre

TRAVELLING IN AMSTERDAM

Transport is the first thing you might worry about it, especially if your accommodation seems like a long trek away after being on a train or plane. Amsterdam has taken the stress out of travel, though; you just need to hop over the road to the tourist information office to get yourself a travel card that will give you unlimited travel for one, two or three days, costing around £15 ($20), £20 ($25) and £25 ($31) respectively. The trams are so easy to navigate – there are stops all over the city and out into the suburbs – and your ticket will also allow you unlimited use of the metro while it's valid, too. However, if you want to travel like a local, you'll find bikes to rent all over the city.

There is so much to do in this bustling city – you won't get bored!

ROTTERDAM

WELKOM TO THE CITY NUDGING AMSTERDAM ASIDE AS THE NEW DUTCH DESTINATION, THANKS TO ITS ECLECTIC ARCHITECTURE AND DIVERSE FOOD SCENE

As a major port city in the south of the Netherlands, Rotterdam is set apart from other Dutch cities by its eye-catching and modern postwar architecture and design. At best it can be described as outrageously eclectic, with styles ranging from the traditional gabled houses dating back to the 17th century, to the curious and iconic cube houses of the 1970s, all muddled in with a touch of maritime flair.

This hip and artistic city boasts a huge range of attractions both in and around the city centre, with a buzzing nightlife scene and numerous independent shops nestled among countless diverse and unique eateries. Both the city and food scene are hugely diverse, with foods to satisfy every discerning palate. Many restaurateurs take pride in offering sumptuous meals using seasonal produce from local suppliers, meaning that the food served in many establishments not only tastes amazing but supports local Dutch growers and reduces the city's carbon footprint.

Fittingly, given the city's reputation for gastronomic greatness, Rotterdam boasts an impressive monument to food in the form of the Markthal. Boasting over 100 artisanal food stalls and numerous restaurants, the Markthal is impossible to miss due to its sheer size, not to mention the incredible mural that adorns its interior walls. Designed by artist Arno Coenen, this floor-to-ceiling masterpiece is the largest artwork in the Netherlands.

Art and culture have always been central pillars of the Dutch identity, and Rotterdam proudly boasts a number of museums, including the Maritiem Museum, the Van Nelle Factory and even the Dutch Pinball Museum. No trip would be complete without a trip to the Het Nieuwe Instituut, where you can experience many interactive exhibitions on fashion, music, architecture and dance culture.

Having immersed yourself in Rotterdam's history (including a look around Sint-Laurenskerk, the only building still standing from Rotterdam's medieval centre and home to the Netherland's biggest church organ), it's time to walk down the Witte de Withstraat. Stretching from the Maritiem Museum to the Museumpark, this district is the beating heart of the city's artistic scene, dotted with theatres, galleries and stylish terraces and cafes. For something stronger than a coffee, beer connoisseurs can discover the delights of the De Pelgrim city brewery and sample some authentic Rotterdam beer!

If you get tired from all that walking, it might be time to put your feet up and embark on an all-you-can-eat pancake boat tour. This will enable you to take in the impressive skyline while seeing how many pancakes you can eat during the 75-minute cruise.

Travel in and around the city can be done via metro, tram and water taxi, or for those wanting to embrace the culture there are bicycles for hire. With Eurostar now offering direct trains daily from St Pancras International to Rotterdam Centraal, in just over three hours you could be enjoying a refreshing Genever (a Dutch botanical gin) on one of the city's many waterside terraces. Proost!

Useful sites
rotterdam.pannenkoekenboot.nl/en
euromast.nl/en/euroscoop-experience
eurostar.com/uk-en/train/netherlands/london-to-rotterdam

Essential information

Hire a Felix electric bike and take a tour of the city's street art and hidden murals.

Best time to visit June to September, when the weather is warm and several festivals are also held

Currency € · Euro

Time zone UTC+1

WEST

BRUGES
HISTORY, CULTURE AND GREAT FOOD MEET IN THIS FAIRY-TALE TOWN

Take a walk at dusk to see Bruges in a whole new light

With Flemish buildings lining the streets, narrow alleyways and little stone bridges over the Dijver, Bruges is more than picturesque – it is straight from the pages of a fairy tale. It's the perfect setting for classical paintings, something that the likes of Jan van Eyck realised. So why not head to Bruges and find out for yourself?

The first thing you'll notice about the city is its beauty, but staring at buildings will get old eventually. Never fear, there's plenty to do besides wandering the streets and drinking in the medieval atmosphere.

Perhaps best known is the Markt, one of the town's main squares, and it's where most visitors head on their first day. From here, streets lead off like spokes to other parts of town, but it's here that you'll see its most famous building – the Belfort. Made famous by films like In Bruges, you can climb the 83-metre (272-foot) tower and, for a small fee, get a quick history lesson and a fantastic view over the rooftops. Other museums include the Archaeological Museum, Choco-Story (for all those chocoholics) and the Gruuthusemuseum, which focuses on the history of Bruges. You can even visit the Frietmuseum, all about the history of Belgium's famous fries, from potato to plate.

Of course, the Belgians are known for other foods, and you'll find them all in Bruges. The smell of fresh waffles wafts down the main streets, while cafes and bars litter the town. And while we're on the subject, no trip to Bruges is complete without a visit to the Halve Maan Brewery. Tours start from around £10 ($13) for adults and include one of the brewery's beers at the end. If you don't want to go round the brewery, you can sit in the courtyard and enjoy the Sun as you sip.

Getting to Bruges is pretty straightforward, with a direct train line to Brussels, and everywhere in the city centre can be reached on foot. In fact, some of the best days you'll have will be poking around the back streets and walking along the canals.

"The smell of fresh waffles wafts down the main streets"

Useful sites
www.visitbruges.be/en
www.visitflanders.com/en/destinations/bruges
www.halvemaan.be/en

Essential information
Belgium is a bilingual country, but Bruges is in the Flemish-speaking part. It's a difficult language to learn, but don't worry – most people will speak English!

Best time to visit All year round
Currency € · Euro
Time zone UTC+1

The Grand Place has incredible sights in every direction

BRUSSELS

CULTURAL AND ARTISTIC WONDERS SPROUT UP EVERYWHERE IN THE BELGIAN CAPITAL

For such a small country, Belgium is a major player on the European stage. Brussels is the seat of power for the European Union, and the Benelux group (Belgium, Netherlands and Luxembourg) has always been among the first to get involved in pan-European projects. As the capital of Belgium, Brussels therefore has a major reputation to uphold and it does that with aplomb, thanks to its gorgeous buildings, incredible art and, of course, wonderfully crafted beer and chocolates.

Brussels is the joint home of the European Parliament. For those interested in tracing the path of continental relations, the House of European History and the Parlamentarium are fascinating and interactive.

Don't spend too long getting to grips with EU history, however, as there is a wealth of beauty to discover. Spectacular sights include Grand Place, the city's central square, which hosts a biennial flower carpet exhibition. Grand Place is surrounded by the beautiful city hall, guild houses and the Museum of the City of Brussels. This last building is one of Brussels' most-visited attractions, an example of Gothic architecture holding multiple artistic exhibits. It was originally a bread market, before becoming the home of the Duke of Brabant.

There are plenty of other examples of fine architecture and interesting museums to explore around the city. The Costume Museum highlights the very best of the lace industry that Belgium dominated from the 16th century; the art nouveau Old England Building houses the Musical Instruments Museum; and the Royal Museum of Fine Arts should also be high on any visitor's list.

Possibly the two most striking buildings in the city could not be more different. The Notre Dame du Sablon is a 15th-century Gothic cathedral, standing elegantly with ornate arches and spires, while the Atomium is a 102-metre (334-foot) metal structure built in 1958 and designed to look like an iron crystal magnified 165 billion times. The Atomium holds activities for kids, Belgium-oriented exhibitions and offers panoramic views of the city.

Botanical gardens are also big in Brussels, with La Botanique and the Parc du Cinquantenaire both being highlights. And no trip to Brussels would be complete without sampling some of its most famous exports. There are numerous breweries around the city to enjoy a tour of while sipping a cool beer, and Neuhaus, Galler, Passion Chocolat and Wittamer are some of the city's most celebrated chocolatiers.

Brussels may not seem the most glamorous city on the surface, but look past the stuffy reputation of the European Parliament host and you'll find a city packed with some of Europe's most amazing architecture, yummiest treats and spectacular art.

Useful sites
www.visit.brussels/en
www.brussels.info
www.introducingbrussels.com

Essential information

Although Belgium is a multilingual country, Brussels is predominantly French and Dutch-speaking.

Best time to visit Every other August for the flower carpet

Currency € · Euro

Time zone UTC+1

WEST

VIENNA

IMPERIAL PALACES, BAROQUE STREETSCAPES AND ARTISTIC MASTERPIECES DEFINE AUSTRIA'S CAPITAL

Situated on the Danube River, this spectacular city has been home to some of the greatest minds, from Mozart and Beethoven to Sigmund Freud.

Much of the city's grandeur is a lasting legacy of the powerful Habsburg Monarchy. Schönbrunn Palace, their summer residence, is a must-see with its pristine gardens and stunning interiors. Take a quirky horse-drawn carriage through the beautiful gardens or wander around the tranquil fountains.

Next to the palace you'll find Vienna's zoo, or Tiergarten Schönbrunn, which is home to red pandas, jaguars, tigers and much more – if you get the Vienna Pass, both the Zoo and Palace are included in the price.

In the centre of the city you will find the Vienna State Opera House (Wiener Staatsoper), which is one of the leading opera houses in the world. Each season, the state opera house offers around 350 performances of more than 60 different operas and ballets, from world-class artists to the permanent ensemble who perform various operas, including Cinderella and Giselle.

Get dressed up and spend an evening at the opera for a truly Viennese evening of opulence and sophistication. Tickets for the opera can start as low as £11 ($14.50), so it is definitely worth going for the experience, even if you don't think opera is your thing – you might be surprised. Each seat has a small screen with English subtitles to help you follow along if you don't speak the language, too.

The Spanish Riding School is another must for any trip to Vienna. Even if you just take a wander through the stunning buildings where it is situated and catch a tiptoed glance at the training arena, you won't be disappointed. The Spanish Riding School is the only institution in the world that has practised for more than 450 years. There are various tours and events that you can buy tickets for, from the morning training sessions to more lavish shows – it's a worthwhile and unique experience.

The city's museum quarter Museumsquartier) features the Leopold Museum, with its numerous works by Schiele; the popular Museum of Contemporary Art; and the Kunsthalle, which is an array of restaurants, cafes and bars that make this area of the city an essential part of your trip.

If you have had your fill of visiting the bigger museums and galleries, then why not venture to the Sigmund Freud Museum? This unique and permanent exhibition is located in the former living quarters and office of Freud, and is a presentation of the great mind's life and work.

Vienna is known for its sumptuous coffeehouse culture, where decadent coffee is served on silver trays alongside delicate cakes and sweet treats. You can't visit Vienna without trying Sachertorte, which is a chocolate cake created by Franz Sacher in 1832 for Prince Wenzel von Metternich in Vienna. The chocolate cake has a layer of apricot jam in the middle, and is topped with a shimmering chocolate glaze. It is one of the most famous Viennese culinary specialities.

If sweet treats and creamy coffee aren't your kind of thing, try heading to a traditional Vienna pub and quietly drink in the atmosphere while you enjoy a Wiener schnitzel or warming goulash washed down with a stein of beer.

Useful sites
www.viennapass.com
www.wien.info/en
www.viennaconcerts.com

Essential information

The Vienna Pass is an essential purchase if you plan on visiting a few attractions, and includes the open-top buses.

Best time to visit
All year round

Currency € · Euro

Time zone UTC+1

You could spend your whole trip just walking the streets of this stunning city, enjoying the beautiful buildings

Hohensalzburg Fortress sits above the Old Town and offers stunning views

SALZBURG

MOZART, MARIA AND MORE IN AUSTRIA'S MUSICAL METROPOLIS

You'll probably recognise bits of Salzburg even if you've never been before. It's thanks to *The Sound of Music* – not only was the once-highest-grossing movie set in Salzburg, but most outdoor filming took place in the Austrian city, too. Follow the story of Maria von Trapp on one of the fun *Sound of Music* tours to the various locations, and join the playful crowds walking around the Mirabell Gardens singing 'Do-Re-Mi'.

There's more to Salzburg's musical heritage than singing nuns. The Hagenauer Haus in Getreidegasse is better known as the birthplace of Mozart and is now preserved as a museum about the world's greatest composer. Amble through the rooms of a middle-class 18th-century family home and see the child prodigy's first musical instruments. Mozart's second Salzburg home on Makartplatz was destroyed in a World War II air raid, but it has been lovingly rebuilt and opened to the public as a second museum, the Mozart Residence. Don't miss the pianoforte at which the genius worked. In addition, every evening you'll find concerts featuring the work of the city's favourite son, with jazz and modern music bars providing an alternative for those who have had their fill of Wolfgang Amadeus. Daylight hours have harmonies and melodies floating in the air as classical music drifts from open windows and street performers busk and sing for spare change. For the best choice of entertainment, visit during the summer Salzburg Festival, when concerts, plays and operas are performed in every possible space across the city.

Beyond Salzburg's musical claims to fame is the Hohensalzburg Fortress. You can't miss it – it's the white castle that towers over the city atop the Festungsberg hill. The fortress can be reached via a steep path – reward yourself with a slice of strudel later – or with a sedate ride on the funicular railway. The views over the baroque Old Town are magnificent, and a chance to spot some of the other sights to tick off at your leisure. Must-sees include Salzburg Cathedral and Residenzplatz public square, Nonnberg Abbey, the trick fountains at Hellbrunn Palace, and the moving wrought-iron memorials in St Peter's Cemetery.

Salzburg prides itself on being the 'Stage of the World'. and with an unmatched musical heritage and a stunning backdrop to perform in front of, it's hard to disagree.

Useful sites
salzburg.info/en
visit-salzburg.net
austria.info/us/where-to-go/cities/salzburg

Essential information

The Salzburg Card is a worthwhile investment, offering you free or discounted entry to many of Salzburg's must-see sites.

Best time to visit All year (depending whether you like Sun or snow)

Currency € · Euro

Time zone UTC+1

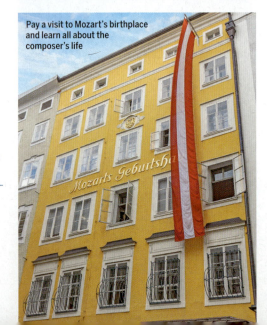

Pay a visit to Mozart's birthplace and learn all about the composer's life

WEST

BERN

WHEN COMPARED TO OTHER CAPITAL CITIES, BERN IS RELATIVELY SMALL, BUT WHAT IT LACKS IN SIZE IT DEFINITELY MAKES UP FOR IN CUISINE AND CULTURE

Visiting Bern's neighbourhoods is a good way to start exploring the city. Each one is unique, with its own characteristics, a variety that is reflected in the differing bistros, bars and restaurants throughout the Swiss capital. One thing they all have in common, though, is the easy-going way of life that oozes throughout the city.

Exploring Bern is easy as everything is within walking distance, although a good public transport service is also available. The Old City is a UNESCO World Heritage Site and its medieval architecture has been lovingly preserved. Take a stroll along the six kilometres (four miles) of arcades, which play host to cafes, shops and restaurants. Referred to by the locals as 'Lauben', it is the longest weather-sheltered shopping promenade in Europe.

Like many major European cities, Bern's centre bustles with weekly markets, with different vendors to be discovered around each corner. Stalls laden with cheese, meats, baked goods, fruit, vegetables, honey and flowers are operated by sellers who pride themselves on their seasonal offerings and live by the motto 'fresh and local'. There is even a yearly onion market, the Zibelemärit, which takes place on the fourth Monday in November and is quite the experience (for the nostrils especially).

Over Advent this fairytale city transforms into a food lover's heaven, with not one but five unique Christmas markets all within walking distance from each other and a large skating rink. The gingerbread-scented streets are festooned with lights and decorations as the city comes alive.

However, Bern offers so much more than exquisite food and charming stalls. There is much to see in and around this beautiful city full of narrow streets, historic towers (including the looming cathedral tower) and countless fountains. Perhaps the most intriguing attraction on offer are the three bears that inhabit the Bear Park in the Old City, a location that is free to the public and open 24 hours a day. The symbol on Bern's coat of arms, bears have dwelt in this enclosure since 2009, and it's currently home to Bjork, Finn and Ursina.

A trip to Switzerland would not be complete without embracing its love of cheese, and if time allows the dairy in Emmental offers tourists the chance to learn more about its world-famous produce. With such good quality cheese a fondue is simply a must. Whether you like your cheese of a more traditional slice, filled with truffles or, in a modern twist, accompanied by gin, this Swiss creation can be enjoyed at any time of the year.

Many locals joke that Bern was in fact built on wine; not only does it produce some excellent vintages but much of the Old City is dotted with both large and small vaulted cellars. Many, like the Klötzlikeller, double as restaurants serving up delicious Swiss comfort food. This family run business offers the most fantastic fondues and houses 30 seats under the arcades and 70 in the cellar.

Bern has a huge beer scene, with over 200 breweries and microbreweries registered in the city. Tours are available throughout Bern, where you can learn, sample and even have a go at brewing yourself. A bit of Dutch (or should that be Swiss?) courage might be needed before attempting a local tradition: a dip in the Aare.

The clear waters of this Swiss river often teem with bathing locals, and those daring enough to take the plunge are rewarded by the strange sensation of floating past the Munster Cathedral, the Parliament Building and even the Bear Park, where the bears might also be enjoying a dip.

Useful sites
emmentaler-schaukaeserei.ch/en
einstein-bern.ch
kloetzlikeller.ch

Essential information

 Flea markets are hugely popular in Bern, with some held at night.

Best time to visit April to September
Currency Fr, CHf, SFr · Swiss Franc
Time zone UTC+1

©Images: Getty

Small street cafes frequented by locals can be found around every corner, alongside bars, boutiques and cabaret stages, some of which are housed in vaulted cellars

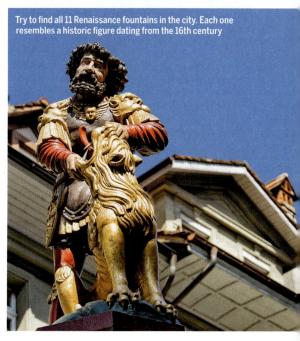

Try to find all 11 Renaissance fountains in the city. Each one resembles a historic figure dating from the 16th century

Grüezi!

There's a tranquillity to Zürich that comes from its closeness to and appreciation of its natural surroundings

ZÜRICH

SITTING AT THE POINT WHERE RIVER MEETS LAKE, THIS SWISS CITY IS CONTEMPORARY, CULTURAL AND KITSCH

Not many would place Zürich high on their list of cities to visit, and in truth Switzerland as a whole is often better suited to nature lovers looking for challenging hikes or to make the most of its Alpine skiing. But it's hard not to fall in love with Zürich from the moment you step onto its idyllic streets. It's a wealthy city, but it's a culturally rich one, too. You will want to make the most of its numerous museums and galleries, key among them being the Kunsthaus east of where the River Limmat meets the lake that gave Zürich its name. With artworks from the Middle Ages through to an exhibition dedicated to Dadaism and surrealism, the Kunsthaus is a great place to start your cultural tour of the city.

From there head west, and wind through the restrained architectural beauty of Zürich's Old Town and the sorts of simple elegance that is so often typified by Switzerland. The city is incredibly accessible by foot, and as you criss-cross over bridges and catch glimpses of the lake, it'll be impossible not to be tempted into one of the city's numerous chocolatiers – how could you visit Zürich and not indulge in the country's most famous export?

But the Swiss city isn't only about its quaint, old-world charm. The wealth of the city born from its popularity with the world's financial institutions has given rise to a hip, contemporary side, and when you're ready to eat it's in its trendy Zürich-West that you'll find yourself. Away from the clock towers and church steeples, the cobbled streets and narrow pathways, Zürich-West is a modern revitalisation of an area once used for factories and dockyards: now it's the bohemian centre of the city, and artists and designers have sought to use the space for more creative purposes. Railway arches have been converted to boutique stores, highway underpasses are cool street food venues, and numerous bars and restaurants will keep you entertained until the early morning.

In that sense you may find a lot of contrast in Zürich: the modern with the traditional, indulgent with the meagre, the natural with the architectural. In any case, it's about time you put it on your list of places to visit.

Useful sites
www.zuerich.com/en
www.zvv.ch/zvv/en/home.html
www.publibike.ch/en/publibike

Essential information

Getting the Zürich Card will allow for unlimited travel on all forms of transport for 24 or 72 hours.

Best time to visit June to August
Currency Fr, CHf, SFr · Swiss Franc
Time zone UTC+1

"The swiss city isn't only about quaint, old-world charm"

WEST

HAMBURG

HOW THE HAMBURGER GOT ITS NAME IS A MYSTERY – BUT WHAT WE KNOW FOR SURE IS THAT HAMBURG IS THE CITY TO VISIT FOR GREAT GASTRONOMIC DIVERSITY!

Germany's second-largest city is drenched in its maritime heritage, a network of canals and old red-brick shipping warehouses fronting its sprawling harbour. One of the biggest and busiest ports in Europe, Hamburg revels in its seafaring history and is famed for dishing up the very best fish from this corner of the globe.

This pedestrian-friendly city is best discovered on foot, but the public transport system is a well-oiled machine, one that proves particularly useful when trying to visit the city's spread-out attractions.

Cycling is another fun and environmentally friendly mode of transport, and with the city's flat terrain you can explore the attractions at leisure and work up an appetite. A good appetite is a necessity in Hamburg; whether it's haute cuisine in a fine-dining eatery, traditional 'Labskaus' in an inner-city restaurant or a snack from a warehouse pop-up, Hamburg offers delicious and sustainable dining to please every pocket and taste.

The Hamburgians pride themselves on their environmentally sustainable ethos, an approach that has seeped into its restaurants and markets, the Zero Waste Cafe serving as a prime example. The presence of several pick-your-own fruit farms just outside the city further enhance the sense that you're visiting a place that is ever conscious of how to keep its carbon footprint under control.

Hamburg hosts ten weekly markets, each with their own unique approach. If you're looking for local produce and craftwork, Ottensen's Eco-Market is the place to go. For a less traditional experience, St Pauli's night market combines diverse food trucks with live music. Flea and antique markets are also hugely popular, but when it comes to a blend of tasty treats and Hamburgian heritage, nothing can rival the Fischmarkt.

Dating back to 1703, it takes place on Sunday mornings along the bank of the Elbe river and attracts locals and visitors alike thanks to a wide array of fresh fish and live entertainment. As dawn breaks the Fischauktionshalle (constructed in 1896) at the heart of the market comes alive with music and the sound of vendors trying to hawk their products and tempt passing revellers from the previous night to one last dance before returning home.

If you prefer a more relaxing start to your day, a walk around Planten un Blomen will not disappoint. This green oasis is home to flowers, exotic plants and ponds. Here you can breathe in the scents of the medicinal herbs and plants in the Apothekergarten (Pharmacist's Garden) and explore the tropical greenhouses filled with an extraordinary array of plants from across the globe. Finish your visit with some afternoon tea in the authentic teahouse in the Japanese garden, the largest of its kind in Europe.

No trip to Hamburg would be the same without a wander down St Pauli's Reeperbahn, home to various sources of entertainment and the city's red-light district. Despite being known locally as 'the sinful mile', the area is filled with hip bars, coffee shops and eateries.

Before you leave the city, pop by the Schanzenhöfe Brewery District and toast your stay with a local craft beer. Speaking of beer, it makes for the perfect accompaniment to a famous north German delicacy – the Fischbrötchen, a freshly baked bread roll filled with cured, fried or baked fish. It can be sourced throughout the city, but nothing beats eating one on the floating pontoons that comprise the 'Landungsbrücken'. Just be sure to watch out for the greedy seagulls!

Hamburg not only has the most bridges in the world but also some of the most picturesque, particularly along Alster Lakes

Essential information

Purchase a Hamburg Card for free unlimited travel on public transport and discounts at many restaurants and attractions.

Best time to visit May to September
Currency € • Euro
Time zone UTC+1

Useful sites
in-guter-gesellschaft.com
stadtrad.hamburg.de/en
hamburg-tourism.de/buchen/hamburg-card

Hallo!

Essential information

🇩🇪 Consider reserving a table if you're visiting during Oktoberfest. It gets very busy and tables fill up fast.

Best time to visit
September to October (to experience Oktoberfest)

Currency € • Euro

Time zone UTC+1

The city of Munich has something to offer everyone, from museums and galleries to beer halls and BMWs

MUNICH

BAVARIAN CUSTOMS AND MODERN CULTURE COLLIDE IN A CITY THAT BOASTS TRADITIONAL BREWERIES, CONTEMPORARY ART AND A FAMOUS FESTIVAL

There's far more to Munich than the lederhosen, dirndl and beer of traditional Bavarian culture, but that doesn't mean you should deprive yourself the pleasures of Munich's traditional side.

Munich's Altstadt, or Old Town, is a great place to start. Here you'll find the city's famous square, Marienplatz. Named after the 'Mariensäule', a column erected in the square's centre to celebrate the end of Swedish occupation in 1638, the square is a must-see for the stunning architecture that surrounds its four sides, most notably its 'new' and 'old' town halls, whose histories date back to 1889 and 1310 respectively.

Wherever you go in Munich, you'll never be far from a brewery, a traditional 'Wirsthäuser' restaurant or a beer garden, key features of Munich's culture of food and drink. Nevertheless, it's worth making a pilgrimage to one of the oldest beer houses in the city: the famous Hofbräuhaus, founded as a brewery in 1589 by Wilhelm V, the Duke of Bavaria. The hall is a mere five-minute walk from Marienplatz, and offers an authentic experience of traditional beer-hall culture. Just ask one of the many regulars whose personal beer mugs are stored in safes at the beer hall!

Of course, if Munich's beer culture is top of your priority list, you'll want to visit during the world-famous Oktoberfest, which attracts more than six million visitors every year. As well as quenching your thirst with stein-fulls of quality German beer, you can enjoy rides, games, stalls and hearty traditional Bavarian cuisine. If you're not a beer fan, consider visiting in the lead up to Christmas instead to experience the city's beautiful Christmas market.

With all this focus on tradition, let us not forget that Munich is a modern, dynamic city too. Head to the Kunstareal museum quarter, where you can see works from Andy Warhol and Damien Hirst, among others, at the striking Brandhorst Museum, and visit Germany's biggest modern-art museum, the Pinakothek der Moderne. Also in the area is the Alte Pinakothek, featuring art from between the 14th and 18th centuries. For those keen on design, make a trip to Villa Stuck, the house of Bavarian painter Franz von Stuck. Don't let its Classical exterior fool you – it's concealing a striking Art Nouveu interior, created by Stuck himself.

For car lovers, a trip over to BMW World is essential. It has a showroom with the latest BMW cars and motorcycles, a museum, and the option to take a guided tour. It also has the bonus of being located next to Munich's Olympic Park, constructed for the 1972 Summer Olympics. Today it is a cultural and social hub, where you can enjoy a concert, ice skate, shop, or simply take a stroll.

Useful sites
www.oktoberfest.de
www.muenchen.de
www.hofbraeuhaus.de

Visiting Munich's world-famous Oktoberfest is a bucket-list experience for many travellers

WEST

FREIBURG IM BREISGAU

GARGOYLES, GHOSTS, AND BLACK FOREST GATEAU – FREIBURG IM BREISGAU IS THE PERFECT SECRET

Deliciously Gothic and rich in culture, no matter the season, Freiburg has you covered. In spring (ish), experience Carnival and the 34 guilds of fools strolling through the city, masked and bedecked in riotous costumes alongside brass bands, flying confetti, and sweets tossed this way and that. In summer, take advantage of the many public swimming lakes scattered around the city, and visit an Eiscafé, with one scoop for less than £1 ($1). In autumn, besides the obvious Oktoberfest, visit a seasonal wine tavern (Straußwirtschaft) for homemade wine and local specialities – watch out for the broom that says it's open! Finally, in winter, visit the Christmas market for a mug of Glühwein and a plate of raclette, try your hand at a spot of candlemaking, or simply wander through the magical Advent evenings.

The daily Münstermarkt is a must-see in all seasons, with 130 stalls in the cobblestone square overlooked by the cathedral. Grab fresh bread or pastries for breakfast, a Lange Rote (literally a long red sausage) for lunch, roasted chestnuts for a winter snack, or a glass of wine at any time of day – even as early as sunrise, when the market sets up. Don't miss the local handicrafts, either, with hand-woven baskets, wooden toys, beeswax cloths, eccentric ceramics, and the Historical Merchants' Hall opposite the cathedral.

Speaking of the cathedral, once you've seen the iridescent stained-glass windows inside, a gift from different medieval guilds, look up and study the outside – there's a wonderful mooning gargoyle carved, legend has it, by a disgruntled stonemason in protest of his meagre wages. The gargoyle appears to be defecating on the heads of the public, and who would want to miss that?

To continue on the trail of the Gothic and bizarre, visit the Old Cemetery, where the grave of Caroline Walter is wreathed in mystery. Her tomb depicts her as a true Sleeping Beauty, and every day for the last 150 years, someone has left fresh flowers – legend says it's her heartbroken lover mourning her for eternity, and in any case, it's a haunting sight to see. For something lighter, visit Mundenhof, Freiburg's free zoo that is open year-round.

To get up above the city, take the Schloßbergbahn for panoramic views of the Old Town, the Vosges Mountains, and the Rhine Valley from the Schloßbergturm's observation deck. A one-way trip is £3 ($4) and a return trip £5 ($6), or walk up using the footbridge from the Schwabentor – there are plenty of scenic viewing points along the way, and it only takes 20 minutes. If you hire a car, don't miss a trip to Schauinsland, the mountaintop reached by Germany's longest cable car. Thirty minutes from Freiburg, the £12 ($14) return ticket is well worth it for astounding views of the Black Forest. Alternatively, from May to October, you can rent high-tech scooters back down into the valley for £26 ($31).

Whatever the weather and whatever your passion, Freiburg has something for you.

Useful sites
schauinslandbahn.de/en
visit.freiburg.de/en
vag-freiburg.de

Essential information

🇩🇪 Purchase the £23 ($28) three-day Freiburg WelcomeKarte for free public transport, including the Schauinslandbahn.

Best time to visit Late June to late September
Currency € · Euro
Time zone UTC+1

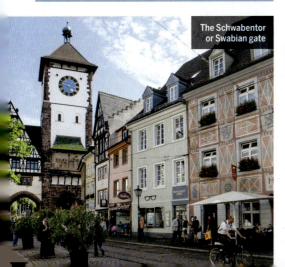
The Schwabentor or Swabian gate

Freiburger Münster, whose oldest bell (Hosanna) dates back to 1258. It rings on Thursday and Saturday evenings or Fridays at 11am

Hallo!

BERLIN

A CITY OF CULTURE AND COOL, GERMANY'S CAPITAL HAS SOMETHING FOR EVERYONE

Berlin's fascinating history as a city formally divided into east and west feels emblematic of a place that always has the potential to reflect an opposite aspect of itself: it has high-culture and pop-culture, historic monuments and cutting-edge architecture, offers both space for calm reflection and a vibrant nightlife, world-famous tourist destinations and little-known secrets for the intrepid to discover. This city will give you whatever it is you are looking for.

Two of Berlin's most iconic landmarks are within a stone's throw of each other and a must for visitors to the city. The Brandenburg Gate, completed in 1791, is not only a great photo opportunity, but a fascinating lens through which to view the tumultuous history of the city, from Napoleon all the way up to the Cold War, which you can learn about in the neighbouring museum. Nearby is the German parliament building, the Reichstag. A stunning juxtaposition of new and old, its historic architecture, which dates back to 1894, is complemented by a striking glass dome set atop it. The dome is open to the public, offering a glimpse into the debating chamber inside, and 360-degree views of the city outside.

A visit to the infamous wall that once divided the city is essential, and we'd recommend you make two stops. First, the Berlin Wall Memorial (Gedenkstätte Berliner Mauer), which extends for 1.4 kilometres (0.9 miles) along Bernauer Straße, shows what the wall used to be like with surviving sections, a watchtower and a documentation centre to provide information on the impact the wall had on the lives of everyday people. For an alternative, but no less significant impression of what the wall and its fall meant to Berlin, check out the East Side Gallery, which has transformed a 1.3-kilometre (0.8-mile) stretch of the wall into an open-air art gallery featuring more than 100 paintings commenting on the political changes the city went through in 1989 and 1990.

If your taste for the city's architecture and history has only just been whetted, then head over to Gendarmenmarkt, a stunning square where you'll get a triple whammy of jaw-dropping buildings in the form of Berlin's 19th century concert house and not one, but two beautiful 18th century cathedrals in the form of the Deutscher Dom and Französischer Dom.

Essential information

Purchase a 'Berlin WelcomeCard' for unlimited use of the city's fantastic public transport system and discounts for some of the city's attractions.

Best time to visit May or October (to avoid peak tourist times)

Currency € · Euro

Time zone UTC+1

"There are a host of interesting neighbourhoods to visit"

Brandenburg Gate is Berlin's most famous landmark and has become a symbol of unity in a once-divided city

WEST

Berlin's Holocaust Memorial was designed by artist Peter Eisenman and engineer Buro Happold

Berlin Cathedral can be found on Museum Island, home to some of the city's best museums

THE HOLOCAUST MEMORIAL

Berlin's Holocaust Memorial is close to many of the city's most popular tourist destinations, so will be easily accessible to any visitor. It consists of 2,711 concrete columns, creating a multifaceted maze for you to wander through and contemplate the enormity of the crime that was the Holocaust. Underground, you'll find an information centre that provides important context via exhibits that document the history of the Holocaust and give you a personal insight into some of its victims. Here, you will also find a room that shows images and short biographies of Jewish victims from across Europe, aiming to give these names a face and story.

Lest we get lost staring into the past, let's remember that Berlin is also a lively, dynamic 24-hour city with so much to do in the here and now. There are a host of interesting neighbourhoods to visit, packed with great food, cool cafes and original bars. Known as the home of Berlin counterculture, Friedrichshain offers cafes, vegan dining, clubs and outdoor cinemas; Kreuzberg, once at the epicentre of the east-Berlin punk scene and with a couple of historic squats still standing, is a hotbed of late-night bars, international street food and fantastic restaurants; and Neukölln is a beacon for artists, boasting galleries, vintage shops and independent bars and cinemas.

The diversity of options on offer to Berlin's visitors is perhaps nowhere better summed up than in its museums. At Museum Island, you can visit five museums that cover 6,000 years of history via artefacts, art and architecture. The most popular museum is the Pergamonmuseum, which houses the Pergamon Altar, taken from the 2nd century ancient Greek city of Pergamon, and a reconstruction of the Ishtar Gate, originally constructed in Babylon in around 575 BCE. The Altes Museum houses a Greek, Etruscan and Roman collection; the Neues Museum contains Egyptian artefacts, including the bust of Queen Nefertiti; and there's also the Museum of Pre- and Early History. Finally, head to Bode-Museum and Alte Nationalgalerie for European

The Christmas market in full swing at the stunning Gendarmenmarkt

sculptures spanning the Middle Ages and 18th and 19th century European art respectively.

As spectacular as these exhibits are, you should also consider museums not on the average tourist's itinerary. Subterranean Berlin (Berlin Unterwelten) is a museum offering tours of the city's underground structures, including abandoned subway stations, air raid shelters from World War II and tunnels used for East German citizens looking to escape to the West during the Cold War – a must for history buffs and dark tourists alike. If you are looking for something really unique, try the Monster Kabinett. Here you'll find a warehouse full of bizarre robotic creatures and beastly sculptures, where actors from the art collective that runs it help create an atmosphere somewhere between museum and haunted house experience. That's not even to mention the computer games museum, the DDR Museum, which gives you a slice of life in the former DDR, and the many other attractions that can be discovered there.

A beacon of cool and culture; a city packed with stunning art and architecture; a place steeped in fascinating history yet with an incredible nightlife: Berlin truly has it all.

The East Side Gallery is an open-air gallery and the longest preserved piece of the Berlin Wall

Useful sites
www.berliner-unterwelten.de/en
www.berlin.de/en
www.eastsidegalleryberlin.de/en

Hallo!

Where old meets new – Luxembourg is a true mix of the ages

LUXEMBOURG CITY

THIS TINY CAPITAL CITY PROVES THAT GOOD THINGS DO COME IN SMALL PACKAGES

You may be forgiven for thinking that the capital city of Europe's seventh-smallest country doesn't have a lot to offer, but you'd be wrong. Luxembourg City in, unsurprisingly, Luxembourg is awash with an array of natural beauty, stunning ancient buildings and bustling modern industry.

The Old Quarter of the city itself is a UNESCO World Heritage site, due to its history as a military stronghold. Luxembourg City sprung up around a heavily-fortified castle, perched atop a hill and enclosed on three sides by the river Alzette. Although the fort itself was dismantled in the late 19th century, it still retains enough features, such as gates, casements and bastions, to qualify for UNESCO status. The casements in particular are a highlight of any trip to Luxembourg, made up of around 21 kilometres (13 miles) of underground tunnels around the city that are great fun to explore.

Home to two fairly sizable rivers, Luxembourg City makes the most of these natural features. Walls of the Corniche is a path that runs around the site of the old fort, offering incredible views of the rivers and city. Such is its breathtaking nature, Walls of the Corniche has been described as the most beautiful balcony in Europe, and there are few who would disagree with that once they've seen it. Another way to get a unique aerial view of Luxembourg is to cross Passerelle, a viaduct that crosses from the south into the centre of the city. Just like Brooklyn Bridge in New York or Tower Bridge in London, Passerelle is an experience all tourists will want to tick off, but don't forget to get a good look at it from the ground as well.

Just a stone's throw away from the site of the old fort is Notre Dame Cathedral. No, not that one, but this Jesuit church is still impressive. Building started on the cathedral over 400 years ago and represents some absolutely gorgeous Gothic and Renaissance architecture, so fans of impressive buildings definitely won't want to miss this.

If you need a bit of time to relax, then Place Guillaume II is the ideal spot, a quaint town square built around a statue of Prince William II – the man after whom the town was named. To the north of the city is Kirchberg, which represents modern Luxembourg. Here you can see Luxembourg's Museum of Modern Art (designed by the architect who created the Louvre's glass pyramid), the unique Philharmonie Concert Hall and, because the city never forgets its roots, Musée Dräi Eechele – a striking fortress around which you can take an interactive tour. The country's generous tax laws have encouraged many multinational businesses to set up shop here, so it is thriving with high-end shopping, hotels and dining. While in Luxembourg City you'll want to try Friture de la Moselle (fried fish from the Moselle river that flows through the city) and Judd mat Gaardebounen (smoked pork neck served with broad beans).

Little Luxembourg City may not be high on many people's must-see destinations, but in terms of history, natural wonders, culture, architecture and food, it really does mix it with the big boys.

Essential information

Luxembourg City is steep so take a funicular to the Kirchberg Plateau and a lift to other districts.

Best time to visit Spring and autumn are the best seasons for nice weather

Currency € · Euro

Time zone UTC+1

Useful sites
luxembourg-city.com/en
visitluxembourg.com
visiteurope.com/en/destination/luxembourg

Moien!

WEST

NICE

THIS METROPOLIS ON THE WORLD-FAMOUS FRENCH RIVIERA OFFERS VISITORS THE BEST OF BOTH CITY LIFE AND BEACH RETREATS

There are few places in the world as spectacular as the Côte d'Azur – the imposing Alpine mountains descend gracefully into fields of lavender and village-topped hills, eventually meeting the Mediterranean coastline. Here, along the southern shores of France, looms the city of Nice. It's one of the most popular holiday destinations, not least because it has absolutely everything to offer visitors, from luxurious beach retreats to a vibrant nightlife.

With its glorious coastline, thriving city and bustling Old Town, Nice is an essential port of call for any trip to the Riviera. As a city, Nice proves that life along the Mediterranean goes on as normal – but with that charmingly laid-back French attitude. Where Parisians sit in cafes and watch the world go by, the Niçois head down to the promenade, enjoying the sea views and slower pace of life. To really experience the Riviera lifestyle, be sure to take the time to sit and relax on or by the beach, sip a Provence Rosé and watch the waves as they tumble towards you.

Like many of France's cities, Nice is a twisting maze of quaint streets, but with a Mediterranean slant. For panoramic views over the famous red-tiled roofs, take a leisurely walk up to Castle Hill. If you'd rather stay in the shade, why not take a wander around Nice's Old Town? The historic quarter is peppered with charming cafes and restaurants, as well as a wealth of spectacular markets to browse. Except for Mondays, the markets run every day – head down to Cours Saleya for an authentic experience, and pick up Niçois produce.

If you're more interested in visiting the city's museums, it's worth popping into the Musée Matisse. Having made his home in the region, Matisse's legacy is hugely celebrated by the area, and the museum holds one of the largest collections of his work. Round the corner from the museum is a serene monastery dating back to the 800s CE, with a beautiful garden.

One other aspect of Niçois life that never fails to excite is the region's cuisine. While the south of France is no stranger to traditional French cooking, it has its own take on food, mixing classic cuisine with Mediterranean charm. Perhaps the most famous French-Mediterranean hybrid is socca, a chickpea pancake. Usually served plain or with savoury garnishes, socca is the highlight of Riviera cuisine. Cheap, quick to eat and delicious, it's the perfect light lunch for anyone intending to spend the day relaxing on the beaches. The south of France's public transport system is excellent, with buses running across the entire coastline, as well as up into the hills and further inland. Likewise, the region is served by a regular train service – trains to the bigger stops run every 20 minutes and cost very little. Nice is the perfect base for day-tripping further into the region – be sure to visit Èze, a charming medieval hilltop town with panoramic views over the entire coast, or experience another world entirely in Monaco.

Useful sites
www.france.fr/en/cote-dazur
en.nicetourisme.com
www.frenchriviera-tourism.com

Essential information

Make the most of Nice's cycle share scheme, Vélo Bleu – it's a hassle to set up, but makes getting around the city quick, easy and cheap.

Best time to visit March to October

Currency € · EURO

Time zone UTC+1

This bustling region offers tourists the best of both lively city life and sedentary beaches

Bonjour!

PARIS

A MECCA FOR ARTISTS AND ROMANTICS, FRANCE'S CAPITAL HAS PLENTY OF GEMS WAITING TO BE DISCOVERED

The iconic Eiffel Tower dominates the skyline around the city

With its reputation as the 'City of Love', Paris certainly has a lot to live up to – but in this sprawling city made up of winding streets and lookalike buildings, it's easy to find yourself stumbling into Paris's most romantic quarters.

Of all of Paris's districts, however, there's no arrondissement quite as spectacular and mesmerising as Montmartre. A suburb built up on the city's steepest hill, Montmartre thrived in the late 19th century as a creative hub, a mecca for all of Europe's greatest artists, including Picasso, Dalí, Van Gogh and Degas. With its cobbled streets, unspoilt vibe and wealth of independent shops and stalls, Montmartre is the living memory of the celebrated Belle Époque, a golden age of French history immortalised in film and literature.

To truly absorb the beauty of Montmartre, it's a good idea to spend a full day – and night – out and about. Visit one of the many crêperies that flank street corners for a chocolatey treat, then allow your feet to take you around town. Any trip to Montmartre isn't worth doing unless you visit the Basilica de Sacré-Coeur, where you'll be granted incredible panoramic views over the city. From here, walk around to the square at the back of the church, where you'll find yourself being hustled and charmed by local artists selling their wares. If you're feeling particularly brave, pose for one of the market's infamous caricaturists!

If you'd rather soak up the art, there are several key locations to visit within minutes of the square – the local Dalí Paris show exhibits some of the kooky artist's key pieces, including one of his Lobster Telephones. Theodorus van Gogh, brother and patron of the celebrated Vincent van Gogh, lived on Rue Lepic, one of the small streets leading down from the Sacré-Coeur, where his brother lived with him from 1886 to 1888. Henri de Toulouse-Lautrec, another of Van Gogh's close acquaintances, also lived around the corner.

Indeed, Montmartre is home to many Parisian institutions, including the infamous Moulin Rouge on one of the main roads through the arrondissement. Despite its less-than-convenient location, tourists flock to this iconic red windmill, keen to capture a photo. The cabaret itself still ranks as one of the best in Paris despite its fame. If you'd rather skip the crowd, however, head across town to Le Zèbre de Belleville for a more intimate, traditional experience.

> *"Life is to be savoured and enjoyed; health and happiness come first"*

While Montmartre might embody most people's expectations of Paris, the city has so much more to offer. Belleville, one of Paris's most diverse suburbs, is renowned for being among the coolest places in the city. Here, take a tour of the local graffiti art on Rue Dénoyez. Nearby is also the famed Père Lachaise cemetery, the final resting place of Oscar Wilde, Edith Piaf and Jim Morrison. An unlikely spot on many tourists' itineraries, the cemetery is nevertheless a popular site and well worth a visit away from the hubbub of the general city.

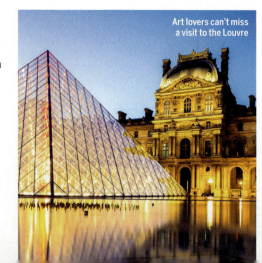

Art lovers can't miss a visit to the Louvre

WEST

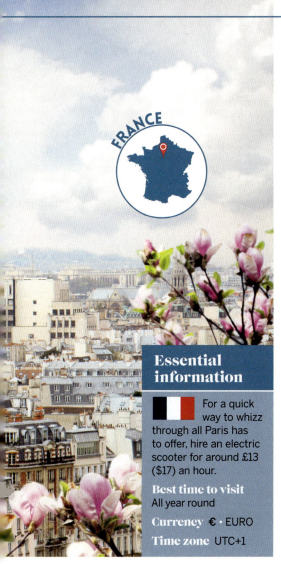

FRANCE

Enjoy the city on foot to see the best of what it has to offer

Essential information

For a quick way to whizz through all Paris has to offer, hire an electric scooter for around £13 ($17) an hour.

Best time to visit
All year round

Currency € • EURO

Time zone UTC+1

Not that Paris is overwhelmed or overworked. In fact, Paris is unlike many of the world's capital cities in that its inhabitants take a very different view on life. Where Londoners or New Yorkers rush around, a week's worth of work to be done in a day, Parisians have embraced a rather different approach to living. Life is to be savoured and enjoyed; health and happiness come first. To visit Paris and to hurry around is very un-Parisian – why not take a tip from the locals? The city is filled with brasseries and cafés, restaurants and bars, so make the most of it. Most arrondissements have their own vibe; once you've found a place you like, sit down, sip on a glass of wine and watch the world go by. Worthwhile visits include La Fée Verte in the 11th arrondissement, an absinthe bar inspired by the Belle Époque. For film buffs, the café featured in the film *Amélie* is down the road from Van Gogh's residence on Rue Lepic.

While Paris has long been hailed as the home of bohemian artists, there is another equally prodigious profession for which the city is an essential port of call. Any chef worth his salt has done a stint here and the city has been the make-or-break for many leading chefs, so naturally it's one of the greatest places in Europe to eat out.

While the city does have its fair share of fancy restaurants, excellent food and experimental cooking is available if you know where to look. Don't be tempted to visit the restaurants that line the key tourist spots – while the sight of visitors dining on mussels and sipping wine at their table might tempt you, often the better restaurants are tucked away off the beaten track. If you're visiting Paris during the week, you'll find that many of the city's restaurants offer cheaper lunch menus, or in the evening there will likely be a fixed menu for a reasonable cost. As well as eating out in Paris, be sure to enjoy the incredible wine on offer. Because France produces so much of the world's best wine, you'll find that the cost of wine is much cheaper than anywhere else on the planet.

No trip to Paris is complete without soaking up the great art – pencil in a whole day to visit the Musée du Louvre. Built on the site of the old Louvre Castle, which was once residence for the French royals, the Louvre is a beautiful mix of old and new, with its glorious palatial complex contrasted by the glass pyramids in the museum's square. Inside the museum is equally spectacular, featuring some of the world's most celebrated artworks including the Mona Lisa, Venus de Milo and the celebrated Liberty Leading the People.

Another iconic Parisian institution that cannot be missed is the Eiffel Tower. Queues form quickly for this attraction, so head over as early as possible to get through security, and ascend before the crowds. With tickets costing about £22 ($28) to travel the 276 metres (906 feet) to the top, it's not the cheapest visit, but the view from the summit is worth it on a clear day. To make the most of your ticket, visit the exhibits, as well as the champagne bar at the top, or take in the views at the second-floor's restaurant.

Useful sites
www.en.parisinfo.com
www.france.fr/en/paris
www.aparisguide.com

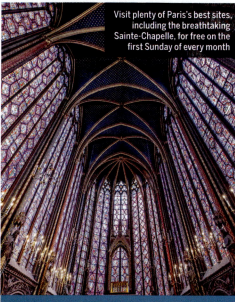

Visit plenty of Paris's best sites, including the breathtaking Sainte-Chapelle, for free on the first Sunday of every month

FREE MUSEUM OPENINGS

With so many incredible sites, galleries and museums to visit, Paris can quickly become an expensive place for tourists hoping to soak up the city's history and culture. However, the first Sunday of every month sees most museums open their doors for free. If you're lucky enough to be in town on this date, be sure to get up early to beat the crowds, as queues are quick to form at the more popular destinations. To make the most of the day, plan an itinerary, using the internet to find out how much time you're likely to spend at different sites. While you can lose yourself for hours in most of Paris's galleries, you may find that half an hour will suffice at other sites. It's worth checking online to find out which museums are part of the Sunday scheme – not all museums participate, and some that do will charge entry at peak summer season.

Vieux Lyon is a Renaissance-era district and home to the city's Gothic cathedral

LYON

FIND OUT WHY THIS MEETING POINT OF TWO RIVERS IS THE CUISINE CAPITAL OF THE WORLD

Essential information

When looking for a bouchon to eat at, try to find the red-nosed marionette and the award 'Authentique Bouchon Lyonnaise' for the true Lyon experience.

Best time to visit
April to May or September to October (to avoid the crowds) or start of December (for the Fête des Lumières)

Currency € · EURO

Time zone UTC+1

While Paris might be the 'City of Love', Lyon has a romance of its own. It's an ancient city, one of Europe's oldest in fact, having been founded 2,000 years ago by the Romans. As France's third largest city, you'd probably expect a hodge-podge of deteriorating terraces and the glass of modern architecture, but Lyon isactually far from such an experience. You'll want to spend a good portion of your time in the city just rambling through its streets, with neighbourhoods like Presqu'île, Croix-Rousse and the Old Town at Vieux Lyon all having the alluring charm you'd expect to see from a city that has grown through the ages.

In doing so, you'll cross over countless bridges, two rivers and climb numerous steps. Battling the latter is handled more ably with the city's two 19th-century funiculars, which pass over narrow streets to take you to the top of the Fourvière hill. Here, you will find an ancient Roman theatre (still used for events today) and the grand La Basilique Notre Dame de Fourvière, which best highlight the age and heritage of the city.

Despite how easily traversable Lyon is – whether by foot or by public transport – at some point you'll need to take a break to stock up on energy for more wandering. Luckily, Lyon is a gastronomical heaven, well-known for its high quality in cookery and offering regional uniquities on top of the usual food fare that France is so famed for. Hunting down one of the city's many bouchons is a necessity – restaurants that offer up meat-heavy, regional dishes like the traditional quenelles (fish dumplings). Meanwhile, charcuteries sell Lyonnaise sausages and it would hardly be a trip to France without a fresh pastry from any of the numerous patisseries.

But the foodie adventures don't end there: you'll want to save space in the stomach to visit Les Halles de Lyon Paul Bocuse, the famed Lyonnaise chef after whom the international and respected competition Bocuse d'Or is named. This market hall is home to dozens of stalls selling the very best produce and food products from across the region.

With renewed vigour, there's still plenty to see. Over 100 murals line the walls of the city, and a tour of these impressive trompe l'œil paintings will have you exploring every corner of Lyon. You'll have a wide variety of museums to explore along the way, too, from a look at the Lumière brothers and the birth of cinema to a fine art collection to compete with the Louvre and even a museum dedicated to miniature models.

Useful sites
www.en.lyon-france.com
www.thisislyon.fr/things-to-do/museums
www.thisislyon.fr/tips-and-advice/transports-in-lyon

Take an evening stroll along one of the city's two rivers – the Saône and the Rhône

WEST

BORDEAUX

WITH ITS BUZZING BRASSERIES AND EXQUISITE VINTAGES, THIS SOUTHERN CITY IS AN IDEAL DESTINATION FOR FOODIES

Undoubtedly the wine capital of France, Bordeaux is dedicated to its moniker. The city is home to many fine wine museums including La Cité du Vin, a cultural space and interactive museum that is solely dedicated to all things wine. The building's unique shape resembles wine being swirled in a glass, and the ethos is not only to celebrate wine but also to educate people about its history and production.

The Musée du Vin et du Négoce de Bordeaux, a much more traditional museum located in what used to be the cellars of Louis XV's very own personal wine merchant, is another must visit for any oenophile. Indeed, the city boasts many wine-related activities, but of course what is wine without food? This is France after all.

Situated in the southwest of a country renowned for its high class of gastronomy, Bordeaux has something to suit every palate. Visitors can enjoy everything from high-class establishments, cosy restaurants and hidden bars, to local producers and farmers markets. What could be more stereotypically French than perusing the numerous stalls of fresh fruit, fish, flowers and cheeses, straw basket in one hand and baguette in the other?

The best farmers markets are located centrally and frequented by visitors and locals alike. Marché des Capucines is hugely popular and can easily be reached by foot or tram from the centre. Another local market is Marché Bio des Quais de Bordeaux, which not only offers top-class oysters, seafood, cheeses and meats but views of the Garonne river and the stunning quays that line it.

Sunrise is the best time to explore the magic of Bordeaux's winding streets and varied architectural history. Bask in the golden hour while the city is still quiet and take a stroll around Bordeaux's cathedral, the Place Pey Berland. This beautiful Gothic cathedral is located in the historic heart of the city, where you can also marvel at several medieval monuments and Haussmannian style of architecture in the Saint Michel district, home to the Saint Michel Basilica. One of the most beautiful in the country, it is thought to have been built between the 14th and 16th century.

In contrast to the elegance of the historic city centre, Bordeaux's port, Bassins à Flot, exudes a young and dynamic feel. It is here that you will find numerous music venues, bars, bold street art and vibrant markets selling all manner of produce. Les Halles de Bacalan is one particularly chic market situated inside an enormous hangar. This gourmet food market hosts numerous artisan stalls, all of which have been specially selected for their high-quality regional products.

One of Bordeaux's more unique features is the Rue Sainte Catherine, the longest pedestrianised shopping street in the whole of Europe. Here you can explore a myriad of boutiques and devour a local delicacy – canelés. These bevelled domed cakes are baked in copper moulds lined with beeswax, which helps to infuse the rum and vanilla custard-like centre with a caramelised flavour.

If you have time to explore outside the city, head north to Saint-Emilion (home to Europe's largest underground church and a treasure trove of delectable food and wine shops), stopping off at Libourne to dive into its remarkable heritage, fascinating culture and outstanding gastronomy. If wine is your thing, visit one of the many Libournais châteaux for some wine tasting before wandering the 600-year-old farmers market held at Place Abel Surchamp.

Useful sites
laciteduvin.com/en
bordeauxwinetrails.com
visiter-bordeaux.com/en/bordeaux-citypass

Essential information

 When visiting any of the markets it is best to arrive early – and hungry!

Best time to visit
May to October

Currency € · EURO

Time zone UTC+1

"Sunrise is the best time to explore the magic of Bordeaux's winding streets"

Diners enjoying the view of Porte Cailhau from Place de Palais. When dining out, especially in the evening, reservations are recommended

Opened in 2016, the eye-catching La Cité du Vin wine museum can be reached by tram, road or metro

NÎMES

THE SOUTHERN FRENCH CITY WHERE EUROPE'S ROMANTIC CULTURES MEET

Nîmes is a meeting point of cultures, history and cuisine, due to its handy location in the south of France. It isn't just the Romans that enjoyed trips to this interesting city, but there is certainly plenty to see in terms of Roman architecture. You will feel as though you are in the heart of the Roman Empire as you approach the wonderfully intact amphitheatre. It is still used today for concerts and local celebrations. In May, the amphitheatre is used for six days of Spanish-style bullfighting (which is controversial, as the bull is often killed. Head to other parts of Southern France to witness indigenous, bloodless bull contests). Another spectacularly undamaged piece of Roman history can be found at the Maison Carrée. Originally a temple dedicated to Gaius and Lucius Caesar, it has since been a house, granary, church and even a tomb.

Since the Roman era, Nîmes has had a turbulent relationship with religion. Place aux Herbes is now a bustling square of coffee shops, restaurants and chocolatiers. However, behind this tranquil setting there lies a story of Nîmes' dark past. There is evidence here of a bloody massacre of Catholic priests and monks that took place during Huguenot rioting in 1567.

As well as Roman history, Nîmes is a fantastic place to experience southern French cuisine and culture. Visit Les Halles de Nîmes and immerse yourself in fresh French food. You will find local people doing their weekly shop, as well as stalls upon stalls of local produce: picholine olives, bream, oysters, and of course wine. Les Halles is also home to food and wine bars, so go with an empty stomach!

The cuisine in Nîmes is very reflective of its location. There are several unique yet typical dishes that are worth trying when visiting the many restaurants and cafes of the town. One dish that you will find all over Nîmes is the brandade de Morue. A purée like substance, made with salt cod, olive oil and a little milk, it's served hot alongside an olive tapenade. You can also snack on some petit pâté nîmois – small pastry parcels filled with veal and pork stuffing. With bullfighting also a local pastime, Nîmes residents take pride in the beef that they eat. Gardianne de Taureau is often a family delicacy. This dish is made by marinating meat in Costières de Nîmes wine, which is then grilled and served with either anchovy butter or a caper, onion and anchovy sauce. It is always served with rice.

Occitanie, in which Nîmes is situated, is a region famous for high-quality vineyards that

> *"However, behind this tranquil setting there lies a story of Nîmes' dark past"*

Essential information

Can you think of a famous material that might be 'de Nîmes'? Find a museum dedicated to denim near Les Halles.

Best time to visit May for the Feria de Nîmes

Currency € • EURO

Time zone UTC+1

How to get there Some low-cost airlines have routes from the UK to Nîmes. Alternatively, the city is around 80km (50mi) from the larger Marseille Provence Airport

WEST

People enjoy an al fresco meal at the Arena Café near the Roman Arena

produce wine for all over the world. Costières de Nîmes, while being part of this illustrious region, has a flavour all unto itself. The place known as the Rhone Delta is the meeting point of the Rhone, Gard and Durance rivers, resulting in pebbly soil and therefore an unusual flavour. When the land is not planted with vines, it is home to rosemary, lavender and thyme. There are plenty of opportunities to take wine tours and get involved in wine tasting both in and around Nîmes. In some cases a car is necessary, but enquire locally to find tours that provide their own transport.

While Nîmes is situated among the beautiful vineyards of the Gard region, there are other local towns and cities that are easily visited from Nîmes. Uzès is a medieval market city located around 25km (15mi) away. With small markets and antique shops, it is a real opportunity to immerse yourself in rural life. The Camargue Nature Reserve is also a manageable day trip from Nîmes and worth the journey to catch a glimpse of the pink flamingos and wild white horses living there. Montpellier is a little further out but remains accessible, with a journey time of around an hour. The town's Gothic and neoclassical architecture is a world away from Roman Nîmes and a fantastic way to explore the next steps in France's colourful history. You can also easily reach several sandy beaches from Montpellier, which will entertain both older and younger travellers.

The Feria de Nîmes is one of the largest annual festivals in France. It is truly a celebration of Nîmes' hybrid French and Spanish culture, where you can watch bullfights, listen to brass bands (peñas), dance the Sévillane, eat paella and watch jousting in the fountain. The celebrations are based around

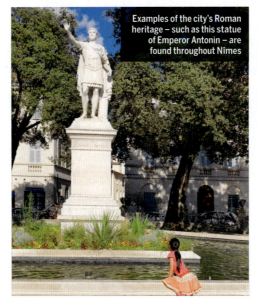

Examples of the city's Roman heritage – such as this statue of Emperor Antonin – are found throughout Nîmes

the Christian festival of Pentecost, which is celebrated in the churches and cathedrals around the town. Over 2 million people descend upon the town at this time of year, creating a party atmosphere wherever you go. While the Feria de Nîmes is a fun festival for the family, there is something to see all summer in this sunny southern city. Whether you are looking for a tour through history or a wander around the luscious Languedoc wine region, there is plenty to see, do and taste in this ancient city.

Useful sites
about-france.com/cities/nimes.htm
nimes-tourisme.com
visitfrenchwine.com/en/vineyard/visit-the-languedoc-vineyards-wine-tourism

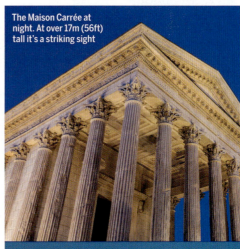

The Maison Carrée at night. At over 17m (56ft) tall it's a striking sight

MAISON CARRÉE

Standing aloft atop an almost three-metre-high podium, the Maison Carrée is one of the best-preserved examples of ancient Roman architecture anywhere in Europe, and is Nîmes' most famous landmark.

Once bearing an inscription dedicating it to the grandsons of the great Emperor Augustus, this fine example of Vitruvian construction would have loomed over the Roman forum of Nîmes, the city a vital outpost for its former rulers, who finished building it in 2 CE.

Since its illustrious beginnings the Maison Carrée has undergone regular and extensive maintenance. The most significant change was the demolition of the buildings once linked to the temple in order to restore it to its original, solitary state. No trip to Nîmes would be complete without a tour of this cavernous monument to Roman ingenuity.